First Impressions Never Lasts

Verses Kindler Publication

Verses Kindler Publication.

Website: www.verseskindlerpublication.com

First Impressions Never Lasts
By: Hemant Bhardwaj
ISBN: 978-81-69248-13-6

1st Edition

Price: INR 299/$15

Disclaimer

First Impressions Never Lasts is authored by Hemant Bhardwaj. The entirety of this published work comprises the original content of the author, who has undertaken diligent efforts in its editing. The characters depicted herein may be fictitious or inspired by real events; however, they are not intended to cause offense or represent any prejudice against any caste or system. Any similarity to the names of actual individuals, locations, or institutions is purely coincidental and serves the narrative. The author bears sole responsibility for the originality of this work; the publisher assumes no liability thereof.

Table of Contents

Pre-Chapter: The Reflection Test

If this were not a book, and we were just sitting across from each other, I would begin our conversation with one simple question. How do you see people?

Not in a philosophical way. Not in a heavy, "deep inner work" way. Just the real, honest, everyday thoughts that run through your mind when you look at someone for the first time.

This reflection exercise is for you to answer that question. You can think of this section as a mirror. Not the kind that shows your face. But the kind that quietly reflects the way you interpret the world. And there's no pressure here. You're not being evaluated, judged, scored, or tested. I'm simply asking you to pause for a moment and notice your own patterns. We all have them.

Later in the book, there's a twist related to these questions, and it lands best when your answers are honest and untouched by overthinking. So give yourself the freedom to respond the way you naturally would.

A Quick Note from Me Before You Start

When you answer these questions, don't try to be correct, wise, spiritual, socially acceptable, or impressive. Don't answer like you're filling out a form at work. And don't over-analyse what I "might" be looking for.

There is no right or wrong here, only how you see people... right now, at this point in your life.

Moving on, as you flip the pages of this book, you will know why I really began the book with this little exercise.

The Reflection Test

You may make notes of the answers in a notebook, on a phone, or even on the margins of this book, whichever is convenient to you.

Just answer instinctively.

1. What is the first thing that you notice about a person when you meet them for the first time?

Their face? Their voice? Their clothes? Their energy? Their confidence? Or is it something random, like their handshake or the way they stand?

2. Do you form an impression of people within the first few seconds?

If yes, what usually shapes that impression?

3. What do you think about first impressions - are they always correct?

4. Did you ever judge someone in the first meeting and realise later that you were totally wrong?

If there's something that clicked, that's your answer.

5. On a first meeting, if someone behaves badly, what do you assume about their behaviour?

That they're rude? Stressed? Arrogant? Going through something?

There's no correct answer, just write your true instinct.

6. How often do you judge people based on their appearance?

Be honest. All of us do this to some extent.

7. Do you think society pushes us to "decide quickly" about others?

If yes, how?

8. When you think about first impressions, whose voice do you hear?

Your parents? Teachers? Friends? Culture? Or your own?

9. Have you ever wished someone had waited longer before judging you?

10. If you had to describe your usual first impression of strangers in one word, what would it be?

Curious? Cautious? Neutral? Friendly? Distant? Skeptical?

Take your pick.

A Final Note Before You Turn the Page

Keep your answers somewhere safe. Don't throw them away. Don't rewrite them. Later in the book, these answers will return, and you'll likely see them through completely new eyes.

For now, let the reflections rest. Let the questions simmer quietly in the background.

Now, let's step into the actual story.

Chapter 1: Challenging the Stigma Around "First Impressions"

Assuming you were raised anywhere close to the world that I was raised in, you must have heard the saying "First impression is the last impression" no less than a myriad of times. It is being thrown around like a physics law, which no one can change, question, or even doubt.

Teachers say it. Relatives say it. Even people who barely know you say it with full confidence, as if they've personally tested the theory on a million human beings.

For a long time, I believed it too. I didn't question it. Why would I? When a belief is repeated often enough, it quietly finds a seat inside you and sits there comfortably. You start thinking you came up with it yourself.

But somewhere along the way, life steps in and asks, "Are you sure?"

I've had plenty of those moments where I asked myself that question. Where I realised much later that my first impression was nowhere close to the truth. Some were funny. Some were surprising. And a few were downright humiliating. But the one that stands out most is something I didn't even recognise as a "first impression story" until much later, it's the impression I formed of my own father as a child.

Back then, he felt like a strict, towering force. The kind of man who noticed everything, how I behaved, how I studied, how I played, even how loudly I laughed sometimes. To me, he wasn't just a parent; he was this rulebook on legs. I remember thinking, "This is who he is. This is what he'll always be."

And then I grew up.

Going away to college changed the dynamic completely. His tone softened. His interrogatives were changed. He no longer asked, "Did you study?" Instead, his questions were full of care. "Are you eating on time?" "How are you managing work?" He did not check my homework anymore. He was checking on me.

It must have been sometime between my childhood and manhood, when neither I nor he ever referred to it, but gradually the man who seemed to me a stern disciplinarian became a friend. He became someone who wanted to hear my ideas, not correct them. Someone who cared less about whether I made the "right" decision and more about whether I was okay. Even now, as a father myself, when I look at him, I don't see the strict man from my childhood at all. I see someone lighter, warmer, more human than the version I had built in my mind all those years ago.

And here's the most amusing part: I didn't change him. He didn't change himself. What had changed was the level of information that I possessed.

The longer I knew him as an adult, the higher the distance I allowed myself to see him beneath the page, the more my impression was rewritten. And that was when I realised that if I was so blind about a person, I know best in the world, how blind I can be about a stranger I interact with for ten seconds.

That's really where this chapter begins.

The belief that "first impressions are final" sounds neat and convenient, but it simply doesn't stand the test of real experience. Human beings are too complex, too layered, too unpredictable to fit inside a single snapshot. Yet we still insist on deciding who they are before we've even heard their story.

Most of this pressure, by the way, doesn't come from within. It comes from society.

We've absorbed the idea that people must "make an impact" instantly, as if the human mind is a high-speed camera that captures the truth in one click. It's a strange expectation. We don't commit to buying a mattress without lying on it multiple times, but we commit to an opinion about a person in a few seconds.

And what's worse, we don't even question it.

We carry these little hand-me-down beliefs from generations before us. A human being in the past must have come up with the saying that first impression is the last impression, and everybody just passed it on like a family heirloom no one wanted, but everybody had.

But when we allow ourselves to reason a little, the question comes up: how can one look, one countenance, one introduction, one emotional moment make up all the character of the person?

It can't.

Yet that's exactly what we do every day, judge based on appearance, or the tone of someone's voice on a tired afternoon, or one awkward conversation they didn't even mean to have that way. With the fragments of information, we create whole stories in our minds.

But here I would like to stop a moment and say a few words about what most folks overlook: most of our first impressions are not about the other individual. They're about us.

They are a part of our childhood. Our worries. Our insecurities. Our previous experiences. Our cultural conditioning.

Assume that first impressions last. My honest issue with it is not that it's wrong, it's that it's lazy. It gives us a shortcut. Instead of getting to know someone, we rely on old ideas borrowed from collective behaviour. We assume that if society has believed something for a hundred years, it must be correct. But collective behaviour isn't always wise. Sometimes it's just old.

Had I just blindly adhered to such a belief, I would never have given myself the chance to come back and see my father as an adult. I would have stuck to the old-school version of him and never gotten the individual who he later became to me.

This is why I encourage people to form their own impressions, not the ones society hands them. You can't judge anyone well if you're judging from someone else's lens. And you definitely can't understand another person if the only tool you're using is a belief you inherited, not one you discovered.

That's the real problem with first impressions: they're rushed, incomplete, and heavily influenced by everything except the truth.

It is, however, only the start of the discussion. What is interesting is to explore more about the process our brains are using to simply leap into these conclusions, the types of stories that we make up in our heads, and why it seems so easy to be so very wrong.

Our minds do not even take ten seconds to form an opinion. The whole judgment sometimes occurs in the time of walking towards a person. A head tilt, a scowl, we suppose, is directed at us. A smile that we suppose is fake. A handshake, too firm or too soft. We create all the characters out of such minute signs. The tapestry of our beliefs weaves a framework for our thoughts, guiding us along the paths we've traveled in our life's journey.

And in truth, even half the time, the impression we present gives more about ourselves than it does about the other.

I began to observe this trend in myself. And there were occasions at some point that I encountered someone on a day when I had already been irritated or stressed out. My thoughts were sweltering, my moods were soaring, and without even having noticed it, I would think that the person facing me was irritating or pompous or impolite. However, later, when it was a calm day, I saw the same person and thought, Why did I imagine this person to be like that? Turns out, they weren't. I was.

For instance, we often find ourselves making snap judgments about others while they navigate their daily lives, whether it's someone not driving as skillfully as we'd expect or someone idling at a traffic light instead of being productive. But when we finally make it home and take a moment to reflect on that critical voice inside us, we realize something intriguing. It was as if our mind was engaging in a dialogue with our better judgment. In simpler terms, the simple routine of driving transformed into a conversation between instincts and logic, shedding light on the nuances of judgment and self-reflection.

That is the bad thing about first impressions, they hardly have to do with what is going on at the time. They are determined by what is already going on in us.

And yet, we are led by society to believe those snap judgments. You can find it everywhere in workplaces, in friendships, in the neighbourhoods, as well as in family meetings. People whisper things like, "I didn't like his vibe," or "Something about her didn't sit right with me," as if intuition is a fact. But intuition without understanding is nothing more than a guess dressed nicely.

Let me give you a simple example. Have you ever met someone who appeared arrogant at first glance? You see their straight posture, or the way they speak confidently, and your mind goes, "Ah, this person is full of themselves." But later, when you get to know them, you realise they're not arrogant, they're just shy, or anxious, or extremely self-conscious.

Shyness often wears the mask of arrogance. Anxiety often looks like rudeness. Overthinking often sounds like indifference.

But you only discover that when you give someone a second impression, a third impression, or better yet, no forced impression at all.

One thing people rarely talk about is how appearances trick us. We assume someone who is well-dressed must be competent. Someone who laughs loudly must be friendly. Someone who looks tired must be careless. Someone who hesitates must be weak. Someone who doesn't smile must be cold.

And that's the thing, we make these assumptions based on a single incident, a single moment, a single expression. As if a person's entire life has been reduced in to the snapshot of the exact two minutes, we happened to interact with them. It's almost unfair when you think about it.

But at the same time, I understand why we do it.

Our minds look for shortcuts. We want to categorise people quickly so we can decide whether they're safe, trustworthy, likable, and reliable. It's a survival instinct that got mixed with social conditioning and turned into an everyday habit.

Here's where the real trouble begins: Instead of forming impressions from our own experiences, we often rely on "borrowed beliefs." Things society has repeated so many times that we accept them as a universal truth.

One of the most common borrowed beliefs is exactly what we're talking about: "first impressions are lasting." It's repeated so frequently that people don't even question it anymore. But here's the thing: if you judge someone only based on the first few seconds, what you're really doing is copying an old belief system that may not even match your own personality.

You're not judging someone based on your understanding. You're judging them based on someone else's fear, or caution, or old-fashioned logic.

That's like wearing a pair of glasses that belongs to someone else and wondering why the world looks blurry.

This is why I always tell people: If you want to judge someone, which we all do, even when we pretend, we don't, then judge them with your own clarity, not society's borrowed instincts. You can't understand another person unless you genuinely understand the lens you're looking through.

Sometimes the lens belongs to our culture. Sometimes it belongs to our past. Sometimes it belongs to our insecurities. And sometimes it belongs to our parents and their parents and the generations before them.

You have to ask yourself: "Is this impression mine, or is it inherited?"

It did not sink in on me until I became a father myself.

I recall that I saw my own children and realised that the image of my father that I had constructed in my childhood was not his complete reality. It was just my childhood lens. He wasn't rigid. He was protective. He wasn't harsh. He was also inexperienced in the same way that I am now sometimes. He wasn't distant. He was attempting to learn about parenthood by trial, just as I am.

The fact of that realization got me considering the number of people I have wrongly judged because I would look at them in the wrong light.

Had I lived my life by just basing my judgment on my initial impression of my father, I would have missed out on the kind of person he became, and I became together with him.

And that is what made me really question that dogma: first impression is the last impression.

It's not just inaccurate. It's limiting. It closes the door even before the individual has even knocked.

Every person will have a point when they will realise that their first impressions are so inaccurate. It may not occur at a very young age, but it comes at one time or another. In my case, it was the time when I began to notice how people transformed in my mind as time went by.

There were colleagues who I found to be too quiet, until the time when they made the funniest joke in the room. I had friends who appeared to be far off until I realised that they were just shy. And there were occasions when I have judged a person by a single incident and found out later that it was just one of their bad days, not their complete personalities.

The further I looked, the more I could see that people are now in a constant movement, emotionally, mentally, even spiritually. No one remains the same as themselves at all times. Their looks will vary according to the time of the day, the circumstances, the past that they are bearing, and the wars that they are waging silently.

But our first impression doesn't see any of that. It sees only a moment, not a life.

That's what makes first impressions so fragile. They crack open the moment you add real information. The moment you hear someone's story, even a small piece of it, the illusion breaks and the truth start settling in.

I remember someone telling me once, "If you want to understand a person, watch them when they don't realise, they're being watched." At first, I laughed it off; it sounded like something a detective would say in a movie. But over the years, I realised the deeper meaning behind it: People reveal their real selves when they're not performing.

First impressions are a performance, ours and theirs. We're both trying to look composed, confident, relaxed, and intelligent, all at once. No one is their actual self in those first few minutes.

That alone should be enough to stop us from taking those early judgments so seriously.

But society loves neat, simple rules, even when they're shallow. The world wants quick labels, quick opinions, quick judgments. "Tell me who this person is so I can place them in a mental drawer." It makes things feel tidy. But people aren't neat. They're messy and layered and wonderfully unpredictable.

If you've ever taken the time to truly get to know someone, you'll know exactly what I mean. The version you meet first is rarely the version that stays.

Let me go back to my story about my father for a second, because it's the clearest example of this for me. As a child, I saw him through the lens of discipline and authority. As an adult, the lens softened. And now, when I look at him, I don't see the "strict father" at all. I see a man who was doing his best, a man who evolved, a man who changed with time, and a man who allowed me to change as well.

The truth is, our impressions of people shift as we grow. When you're young, you judge with limited understanding. When you're older, you judge with lived experience. The second version is always more accurate, because it's informed by your own growth.

This is why I genuinely disagree with the belief that "first impressions are lasting." They aren't. They're temporary placeholders. They're guesses. Sometimes they're wildly wrong guesses. People talk about that line as if it's a fact, but it's more like an old superstition passed down without question. A habit disguised as wisdom.

And here's the part many people overlook: If your impression of others never changes, it means you aren't growing.

Every time you evolve, your lens evolves too. And you constantly evolve in every moment with new information that your brain possesses.

That's the beauty of human relationships; they shift with time. Sometimes they deepen. Sometimes they fade. Sometimes they surprise you in the most unexpected ways. But none of this can happen if you freeze a person in your mind based on the few seconds when you first met them.

The biggest gift you can give someone is the freedom to be more than your first impression of them. And the biggest gift you can give yourself is the freedom to update how you see the world.

I've reached a point in life where I don't rush my impressions anymore. I don't rely on the surface. I wait. I observe. I listen. I allow space for people to reveal themselves. And honestly, it's made my connections deeper, my conversations richer, and my heart a little softer.

Because when you stop judging people too quickly, you start understanding them more sincerely.

Once you slow down and let go of the rushed judgment, you start noticing details you would have missed earlier. The kindness in someone's voice. The hesitation behind someone's confidence. The vulnerability hiding under someone's silence. You realise how many stories people carry that you never knew about.

And that's what breaks the myth of first impressions completely.

By the time you reach the end of someone's story, or even a small part of it, you can't believe you ever thought you knew them in the first two minutes.

As I wrap up this chapter, I want to leave you with something simple, something I try to follow myself: Let people surprise you. Let them show you the sides you didn't expect. Let them reveal the layers they're not comfortable showing right away. Let them grow in your eyes. Let yourself grow with them.

The world becomes a much kinder place when you stop locking people into the version you met first.

And as we move to the next chapter, I want you to carry one question with you, not as homework, but as a quiet companion: If first impressions can be so wrong, then what exactly is happening in our mind when we meet someone?

Because the answer to that question opens the door to understanding perception itself. How we see. Why we misunderstand. And how our brain takes shortcuts that often mislead us. And that's exactly where we're heading next.

Chapter 2: How Perception is Formed - The Science Behind What We See

I've always wondered why the mind reacts so fast when we meet someone new. It doesn't ask our permission. It doesn't stop to think. It simply jumps to a conclusion and hands it to us as if it's the truth. The lessons of first impressions were too vivid for me not to think more deeply about where they originated from. I quickly realised that the answers I created within myself were not outside of myself, but inside of myself.

This became clearer to me through an example during college. I remember a girl, not for her physical beauty, but for the image I built of her in my mind.

When I first saw this girl, I built an entire character around her in my mind. I interpreted her as being arrogant, picky about her friends, and entirely self-absorbed. None of which was based on anything she actually said. All of it was based on a story I made up in the first few moments.

Now I laugh, thinking that I so easily believed that story. I had no evidence. No real interaction. Just a glance and a conclusion.

As time passed, life did what life does: it gently corrected me. As I spoke to her, my understanding of her grew through honest conversation, without any preconceived ideas. Each time we spoke, the greater my embarrassment grew at the person I had imagined her to be. The person I had pictured was nothing like the real person. She was kind, thoughtful, and simple. She was down-to-earth and had no trace of superiority at all.

That was the first time I realized how rapidly a person's mind can deceive them.

It didn't remain with me due to the nature of what I learned from her, but because it reflected something about me. My perspective of her was not an observation about her at all. It was about me, my own insecurities, my memories of people from school who had seemed "unapproachable," the way I had always interpreted confidence as exclusivity, and the way I projected my own fears onto her silence.

She hadn't created that impression. I had.

It's strange how confidently the mind fills in the blanks when it has very little information. And once it creates the story, it attaches feelings to it, certainty, irritation, and caution.

The funnier part is that it does not happen just with people. I have even had it happen in contexts.

Once, I made an appointment to meet someone. I remember being fully prepared. I was at the right place, at the right time. I was expecting everything to unfold without obstacle. He never showed up. Not a call. Not a message. Nothing. My mind reacted immediately, and the reaction wasn't small. "He doesn't value my time." "He's not a responsible person." "He has no value for his own words." Within a minute, I decided that this person cannot be trusted.

Later, I got to know that the person was extremely sick. Too sick to even reach for his phone.

And suddenly, all those strong judgments melted. What remained was a quiet sense of guilt. Not the heavy kind, just the gentle kind that makes you realise how fast the mind can misread a situation.

Both incidents, the girl in college and the man who didn't show up, taught me the same thing. Perception isn't built on facts. It's built on whatever the mind already believes.

We think we interpret the world as it is. But we interpret the world as *we* are.

I had another experience in my past that supported my newfound awareness of the importance of perception. When I was young, there was a festival celebration in my village, and an elephant was brought to the village to participate in the ceremony at the temple. At the time, I was very young and, like many of the children my age in the village, I had only ever seen pictures of elephants. So, when I saw this gigantic beast walking down the street, it was a mix of excitement and shock. I distinctly recall being transfixed by what I saw; I distinctly remember an ambivalence between awe and fear. It was large and strange.

As my parents made me sit on its back for a ride, I was terrified. My heart was racing, and my breath was heavy, as if I was climbing a mountain. But then, something started to change. I peered through the elephant's eyes, and I could not help but notice its gentleness. I saw how responsive it was to its mahout. I saw how it moved calmly but deliberately. It was the same elephant, same me, same moment even. But my feelings and perception had shifted.

I always thought the elephant had somehow changed for me. But it hadn't. It was I who had changed.

That experience demonstrated more to me about perception than any book could. It made me realize that what we see in another person or situation is never about the moment in and of itself, but instead, it's filtered through everything we have experienced prior to that moment in time, particularly from our youth, even before we fully understood anything about our experience.

We don't begin life with logic. We begin life with emotions.

We identify the feelings of fear or warmth, comfort or discomfort, much before we ever look at ourselves in the mirror. All those feelings get etched within us, like the roots of our entire belief system, and those beliefs quietly shape our perception long before we learn to reason.

Years later, when we meet a stranger, it's not the stranger we see. It's the emotional memory they awaken inside us.

This realisation made me look at my life differently. I no longer just saw what I was reacting to. But I also looked at what those reactions were made of. And whenever I sat with those reactions long enough, I always found traces of my past hidden in them.

The impression I had formed of that girl in college came from childhood memories of feeling out of place around certain groups. The irritation I felt toward the man who missed the meeting came from older experiences of people not keeping their word. The fear I felt toward the elephant came from nothing but inexperience.

None of these impressions came from the actual present moment.

They came from the stored moments inside me.

After I learned this, perception became less of a mystery and more human-like. We don't respond to what is in front of us; we respond to what resembles something within us. And once you see this moving around in your head, something loosens in the way you look at other people.

You stop assuming. You start noticing. You stop concluding. You start understanding.

The world outside doesn't change. The world inside becomes clearer.

The more I focused on those tiny instances and those quick assumptions, and those instant stories my mind was happy to create, the more I realized how perception has very little to do with the outside world and everything to do with the world inside. What I perceived as an instantaneous sense of intuition was my past working away quietly in the background.

It's strange how subtle this process is. You don't feel it happening. You don't hear a sound. You don't notice a shift. One moment you're looking at someone. The next moment, you've already decided what kind of person they are. It's almost automatic. Like breathing.

It wasn't the automaton fact that piqued my curiosity; it was the consistent feeling of reality that accompanied using the automaton. I never raised the question of whether my impression had been caused by what I had seen or what I was carrying inside. I can now say that it took me years to realize how deeply personal perception is etched within our hearts and minds.

When someone walks into a room, the senses do their job/ They collect information. You notice their tone. The way they gesture. How they smile or don't smile. How they hold themselves. How they speak. You notice all of this before you even realise, you're noticing it. But all this information is just the surface. It's not enough to form an impression.

The real impression begins when this information enters the mind and looks for a match. The brain, without asking you, searches through years of emotional memories trying to find something similar. It's almost like an archive that's constantly buzzing beneath the conscious mind. If anything in the present resembles something from the past, even slightly, the brain picks up that emotion and presents it as perception.

That match may be completely irrelevant, but the mind doesn't know that. It only knows how to compare.

Over time, I began to understand that this entire process happens in a sequence so fast and so quiet that we rarely notice it. Everything we sense becomes raw material. The things we see, hear, smell, taste, or touch don't stay at the surface. They are stored, layer by layer, from the earliest years of our lives. Before we learn language, before we know how to reason, the mind is already collecting these experiences and turning them into patterns.

Those early patterns settle inside us as part of our emotional memory. They become our reference points. And as we grow, these reference points quietly shape the beliefs we carry. We don't choose these beliefs consciously. They simply take form as our mind tries to make sense of everything it has gathered so far. By the time we reach adolescence, a large part of our internal repertoire, our storehouse of memories, learnings, and emotional impressions, is already built.

So, when new information enters the mind, it passes through these earlier layers. First comes the sensory input. Then comes the search for a pattern. Once the mind recognises something familiar, even faintly, it interprets the situation through the beliefs that have formed over the years. Only after this interpretation do we feel an emotional response. It might be trust, fear, irritation, warmth, caution, comfort, or even a sudden sense of intuition.

By the time the emotion arrives, the perception is already formed. And the surprising part is that the whole chain, from sensation to memory to belief to emotion, happens automatically. We don't control it. We don't approve of it. We don't consciously participate in it. It unfolds in the background like a reflex.

What made this process even more fascinating to me later was realizing that people had tried to understand this inner movement long before science had the tools to study it. Ancient Indian thinkers had mapped the workings of the mind with remarkable clarity, not through anatomy but through experience. They described the mind as having four inner faculties that shape how we perceive anything: the part that gathers impressions, the part that reacts emotionally, the part that stores memories, and the part that steps in to clarify what is actually true. They were not talking about physical pieces of the brain. They were talking about qualities we can feel inside ourselves even now.

Much later, when neuroscience began to understand how the brain responds to the world, it identified a structure that filters sensory input, a structure that reacts emotionally, a structure that carries our memories, and a structure that helps us pause and think. The language was different, the approach was different, but the pattern was astonishingly similar. One spoke in the language of inner experience. The other spoke in the language of biology. Yet both were describing the same inner sequence that moves through us every time we sense something.

When I noticed this overlap, something inside me lit up with recognition. I could see how these ancient descriptions applied directly to the small moments I had lived. I could see how quickly the mind collects only a few details, how immediately the sense of "I" feels threatened or defended, how easily old memories rush in even when we don't want them, and how clarity arrives only at the end. I had lived this sequence countless times without having the words for it.

It reminded me of a simple moment from work years later. Someone walked toward me looking serious, and before a single word was spoken, I had already braced myself. My mind had picked up a few cues, my sense of self felt the possibility of being judged, and a memory of a similar situation surfaced on its own. All of this happened so fast that it felt like the truth. And yet the person simply asked if I needed any help. The tension dissolved immediately, not because the world changed, but because my mind had finally caught up to the moment. It was a small example, but it showed me how often the mind writes a story before reality has had a chance to speak.

The more I reflected on this, the more I understood that perception is stitched from these four movements inside us: the way we notice, the way we react, the way we remember, and the way we correct. Modern science may describe them as different structures of the brain, but the inner experience remains the same. The first three move quickly, instinctively, without permission. The last arrives slowly, quietly, almost as a second thought. And most of the time, we respond to life before that quiet clarity even gets a chance.

Seeing these two worlds, ancient understanding and modern science, mirror each other made the whole process feel more human. It made me realise that our first impressions are not small mistakes. They are the natural result of an inner system doing its job too quickly. We don't see things as they are. We see them as the mind prepares us to see them. And once I realised this, my judgments softened even further. Not because I suddenly became wiser, but because I finally understood why the mind behaves the way it does.

This is why people often say, "I just got a feeling." The feeling isn't magic. It's memory working in disguise.

I remember watching myself once when I was having a conversation with a stranger. There was something in his manner of speaking that made me uncomfortable. I didn't know why. He wasn't being rude.

He wasn't being unpleasant. But I felt a little guarded. For a few minutes, I kept wondering what it was that he did that made me uneasy in my own head.

Much later, when the conversation ended, and I was able to think about it calmly, I realised that the way he was speaking had reminded me of someone whom I had trusted in the past and regretted trusting. The tone, the rhythm of his speech, his pauses in between sentences, it didn't take much to remind me of someone, and I ushered that experience into the present moment.

The stranger was not doing anything wrong; it was simply my past emerging through the present.

Once you begin to see the pattern, you cannot begin to unsee it; you start to realise how often the people around you seem to react without cause. Someone gets offended, although no offence was meant; someone distances themselves from you when there is nothing threatening in the relationship; someone becomes overly cautious because something reminds them of their past experience.

No one reacts to a situation. They react to what the situation represents to them.

This is why it so happens that two people walking through the same moment often come up with different interpretations. One feels respected. One feels ignored. One thinks it was friendly. The other thinks it was cold. The moment doesn't change. But the meaning each person attaches to it does.

We carry our entire emotional history into every interaction.

And that emotional history forms what I call the inner lens. Everyone has one. Some people realise it. Most don't. But it's always there. Shaping the way we see the world. The way we interpret behaviour. The way we form opinions. The way we judge. The way we react.

This lens is made of everything we've experienced. Our joys, fears, embarrassments, childhood, and disappointments. The voices we heard growing up. The beliefs passed on to us. The moments that shook us. The moments that comforted us. Our lens is just a reflection of everything we've lived.

And because every person's life is different, everyone carries a different lens. Which means everyone sees the same world differently.

Once I understood this, I began noticing something else, too: how often we mistake our lens for truth. We treat our perception as if it were the only accurate version of reality. However, the reality is much more fluid and much softer. While reality exists in the shared world of others, perception is a personal experience. I have observed people join a conversation already in their mind, convinced that the other person would not understand them. So even if the other person was making a genuine attempt at warmth and connection, the person who initiated the conversation still experienced a perceived reality of not being understood. It wasn't that the warmth wasn't there, but rather that they were filtering it through a different lens. The mind sees what it expects to see. There is a level of innocence in this, but there is also a level of sadness. How many beautiful connections do we miss because we think we already know how the event will unfold? How many misunderstandings grow simply because someone's words accidentally resemble an older wound? How many opportunities slip by because past experiences whisper louder than present possibilities?

There's a quiet truth I've come to believe: we rarely meet people as they are. We meet them as our mind has prepared us to see them.

And when that preparation is built on fear, doubt, or insecurity, even kind faces look threatening. When it's built on warmth or familiarity, even strangers feel safe.

This is why first impressions feel so convincing even when they are wrong. They don't come from a moment. They come from a lifetime.

As I understood this, my entire approach to interpreting my instincts changed. I used to think of intuition as a mysterious signal coming from an outside world. Now I treat it as a message from the inside. Intuition doesn't come from nowhere. It comes from patterns the mind recognises faster than the conscious brain can.

But intuition is only as accurate as the emotional history that shapes it.

If your emotional history is filled with fear, your intuition will warn you constantly. If your emotional history is filled with openness, your intuition will trust easily. If your emotional history is balanced, your intuition becomes calmer, clearer.

The inner lens writes the script long before we say our first word.

And the most surprising part? This inner lens was being shaped even before we knew who we were. A child doesn't recognise itself in a mirror during the earliest months. However, it recognises fear, comfort, hunger, and warmth. Those emotions settle in the mind long before logic arrives. They become early building blocks of perception.

So, as we grow up, perception is not what we learn. It is what we discover within ourselves.

The more deeply I understood it, the more my relationship with my reactions kept changing. If I felt uncomfortable around someone, I did not think that there was something wrong with them. I paused and checked what it reminded me of. If I felt like I was drawn to someone, I did not think that they had some kind of aura. I paused and asked myself about what it was in me that was responding.

That small pause shifted everything.

It softened how I looked at others. But more so, it softened how I looked at myself. I was no longer fighting my reactions. I was learning from them. They were no longer mistakes; they were mirrors.

And every mirror showed me a part of me I had ignored.

The more I understood this, the more gently I walked through the world. People became less puzzling. Their reactions were easier to understand. Situations felt more layered, less personal. I began to notice that there is a difference between what happens outside and what happens inside.

I could understand that perception was not about interpretation alone. It was also about connection. Connection between old experiences and new ones. Connection between memory and meaning. Connection between who we were and who we've become.

Once that realization settles, things slow down. Not just physically, but emotionally as well. Reactions become reflections. Intuition becomes insight. Judgment becomes curiosity.

The outer world doesn't look different, but the inner world feels steadier.

And that steadiness is what changes everything.

What changed me the most during this whole journey was not the understanding that perception is subjective; that's something most of us have heard before. What changed me was realising just how deeply that subjectivity runs. It isn't a small tilt of perspective. It's the entire architecture of how we hear, see, feel, and interpret life.

When you realise the mind is constantly using the internal archive as a reference, you will recognize that the way you engage in conversations begins to change. You will also observe how many people are responding to something that is not happening in the present time. A simple question gets received as criticism. A suggestion gets taken as disrespect. A delay becomes a personal offense. Silence becomes a sign of anger. None of it may be true, but their mind connects the present with something old, and suddenly, the emotion feels justified.

I've caught myself doing this too. On some occasions, I became more defensive than needed at someone's feedback. It was not that the feedback was bad or harsh. Instead, the feedback simply had touched an old feeling that made me feel like I wasn't good enough. On some other occasions, a small act of kindness impacted me more than it should have. It was not something extraordinary. However, it had reminded me of a person or feeling I cherished. So, each time, my mind was adding weight to the moment.

It is for this reason that different people interpret the same things differently. People come from different histories. They carry different memories. They have their own share of shadows and emotional residues. Everyone's perception of fear, hope, and longing is different. And because this perception differs, the interpretation of things and moments is different for different people. It totally depends on the person who is experiencing that moment.

As I understood this, it entirely altered how I dealt with misunderstandings. Understanding this changed my way of dealing with misunderstandings. In the past, if I witnessed an outburst or a negative response from someone, I automatically assumed it was directed toward me. Now I take a breath before reaching any conclusion. Sometimes their reaction is not about me at all. Sometimes it's about their own emotional history, their inner lens, not mine. And even when it is about me, it's rarely about the moment itself. It's usually about something that the moment resembles.

This small shift, this pause of awareness, has saved me from unnecessary hurt, unnecessary confusion, unnecessary conflict. It has helped me understand that everyone is moving with something invisible, something unspoken. Everyone is interpreting the world in their own different ways. And they are doing it with different layers of emotions. Feelings that they might not even know are there.

And I'm no exception.

There was a time when I believed I was interpreting situations rationally, that my perceptions were accurate simply because they felt accurate. Emotions are not always accurate but rather compelling. They are loud, self-assured, persuasive, even to reciting something out of a memory that has nothing to do with what you are now looking at.

The more I listened, the more I realised that I had so many times confused familiarity with truth. In case the behaviour of someone resembled something in my past, I responded to the similarity and not the fact. When something reminded me of a previous disappointment, I steeled myself in case anything went wrong. My reactions weren't wrong. They were human. However, they were constructed on relationships that were not visible.

I started perceiving life differently when I realized there is no certainty of the inner process, but rather the outer perception. I understood that objectivity is not an inborn concept. It's something we grow into. It is hard to look at the world without the past taking the present. It is a process of patience to be able to separate what is happening from what your mind is being reminded of. It requires a degree of sincerity to pose a question to yourself of whether you are reacting to the present or to the past.

And it takes bravery to realize that you are not always right in your perception.

Such awareness did not help me eliminate my judgments, but it diluted them. It helped me to be less sure about my suppositions and more interested in the truth. It slowed my reaction and speed to comprehend. My attempts to make opinions ceased immediately. I started letting events unravel. I gave people room to be more than my original perception of them. I gave situations time to show their context and then made a decision about what they entailed.

Above all, I gave myself the space to develop beyond my previous patterns.

The most surprising was the degree of clarity this was able to bring not only to the people around me, but to myself. When you take time to listen to yourself, you will find something about yourself that was silently informing your responses. You feel insecurities that you did not realize. Fears that were silently affecting your decisions are identified by you. You find you have had expectations that you never knew you had been bearing.

And when you see them, then they do not rule you in the same way.

You begin to view the world as balanced. You begin to be more patient with people. You would begin to enter into situations with fewer assumptions. You understand that everybody, including yourself, needs to be given an opportunity to be understood without making the comparison to the past.

It is at this point where perception is first encouraged to change, not through coercion, not through discipline, but by being aware of it.

It is the consciousness that makes you different in the way you walk in the world. It modifies the weight of your reactions. It alters how you interpret the expressions of people, how you interpret the silence of people, and how you interpret their behaviour. Consciousness softens where you were hard, clarifies where you were opaque, and relaxes where you were combative.

The external world does not change a bit. And your inner world is more stable. And due to that, the outside world is different as well.

When I came to this realization, I realised something, simple and yet profound, and it is that perception does not define the world, it defines your dealings with the world. And when you recognize the prism through which you are looking at everything, that makes that relationship deeper and more honest.

That is why Chapter 1 had to be introduced as a prelude. The first impressions are hard to refute unless you are aware of the way you get the impressions within yourself. And now that you have examined this inner process carefully, something significant comes out: that for the most part, what we perceive in others is influenced by what we bear in ourselves.

When the world is always filtered by the history of the mind, then nearly all of our judgments, all our instincts, all our intuitions are in some sense reflections of ourselves.

And that realization leads to the next section of this journey, which is how much of what we think about others is, in fact, just a reflection of our own life, beliefs, and emotional templates.

That's where we go next.

Chapter 3: The Selfie Lens - Seeing Others Through Ourselves

There came a moment when I realised that perception alone was not the full story. Yes, the mind filters what it sees. Yes, memories shape how we interpret people. Yes, our past quietly influences our present reactions. But there was another layer at work. One that was even more deceptive because it felt so natural. That layer was expectation.

I was not just seeing the world through my past. I was also demanding that the world behave according to it.

That realisation came slowly. Through many small disappointments that didn't quite make sense at first. I would walk into conversations already anticipating how the other person would respond. I would enter situations already imagining how they should unfold. I would meet people already deciding how they ought to behave with me. And when reality did not match what I had silently predicted, something inside me would tighten. I would feel let down. Irritated. Misunderstood. Or quietly hurt.

I believed that this discomfort came from people. And I believed in that notion for a very long time. But as time passed, I discovered something deeper. I understood that the discomfort came from a gap. The gap between what I expect and what their reality is.

I began to notice how quickly the mind wants to believe its own predictions. It barely pauses. It barely checks for logic. It wants certainty. Even if that certainty is imaginary. And the moment expectation settles in, perception becomes biased. It happens without us even realising it.

When I expected warmth, even neutrality felt cold. When I expected respect, casual behaviour felt like an insult. When I expected understanding, distraction felt like rejection. When I expected consistency, human fluctuation felt like betrayal.

I was not reacting to what was happening. I was reacting to what I thought should be happening.

This is when the idea of the "selfie lens" became clearer to me. Earlier, I understood that I was projecting my memories onto people. Now I saw that I was also projecting my expectations onto them. I wasn't only reading others through my past. I was also reading them through my desires, my fears, and my personal blueprint of how the world ought to behave.

It became obvious that most of the time, I wasn't really meeting people as they were. I was meeting them as I expected them to be.

And the more I observed this in myself, the more I saw it everywhere.

I saw it in friendship. One person silently expected constant emotional availability and felt hurt when the other couldn't provide it. I saw it in families where parents expected children to live according to inherited beliefs and felt disappointed when they grew into their own people. I saw it in workplaces where managers expected instant excellence and labelled growth as incompetence. I saw it in romantic relationships where one person expected the other to heal their emotional emptiness and felt abandoned when that didn't happen.

Expectation was quietly sitting beneath all these conflicts, shaping the emotional reactions that followed.

What surprised me most was how logical expectation feels in our minds. It doesn't announce itself as imagination. It presents itself as common sense (but then, one idiom, that's always valid, always prevails - "Common Sense is not Common Nowadays"). It convinces us that what we want from others is reasonable. That our predictions are fair. That our interpretations are accurate. And because it feels so reasonable, we never think of questioning it.

But when I started questioning it, I saw something that unsettled me.

I saw how often my expectations had nothing to do with the person in front of me. They were built from my past. From my childhood. From my conditioning. From my fears. From my longing to feel safe, respected, valued, and understood.

I wasn't just seeing others through myself. I was demanding that they function according to me.

And that is where the distortion truly begins.

The more I sat with this, the more I understood why we so confidently believe we are judging others correctly. It is because we are not actually judging them. We are judging how well they fit into our internal pattern. We are measuring them against the emotional blueprint we already carry. And when they match it, we feel validated. When they don't, we feel disturbed.

This is where that idea began to make deep sense to me. That nearly ninety-five percent of what we think we see in others is still us.

Not because others don't have their own reality. But because our interpretation of their reality is built almost entirely inside us.

The mind does not wait for truth. It waits for familiarity. The fastest shortcut it knows is memory. So the moment something feels unclear, it does not pause for clarity. It instantly supplies meaning from the past.

And the mind does something even more surprising. It answers its own questions.

If someone speaks less, the mind doesn't say, "Let me wait and understand."

It says, "He is disinterested," if I fear rejection.

"He is arrogant," if I have felt dominated in the past.

"She is angry," if I grew up around emotional explosions.

"He is judging me," if I judge myself.

"She is shy," if I once was.

The mind is not reading the other person. It is reading itself through the other person.

This is when I began to see how deceptive rationality can be in real time. We like to believe that we are making sensible, logical evaluations of people and situations. But most of the time, we are emotionally charged, distracted, tired, triggered, hopeful, anxious, or defensive. In those states, what we call reasoning is often just the mind protecting its own emotional comfort.

True rationality does not usually happen in the moment of perception. It comes later, when we pause and reflect.

And because we confuse reaction with logic, we misjudge people. We misinterpret intentions. We label too quickly. We trust too fast or reject too fast. We punish people for assumptions we created. And the most dangerous part is that we do all of this while feeling absolutely confident that we are right.

This is how emotional errors quietly shape the direction of our lives.

The friendships we walk away from too quickly. The partnerships we choose impulsively. The people we mistrust without reason. The people we idolise without knowing. The decisions that feel right at the moment but shape years that follow.

And behind many of these choices sits the same silent driver, expectation.

At some point, I began seeing how most of my assumptions were not truths at all. They were probabilities. And probabilities are hard to understand, which an irrational mind cannot understand. Probabilities are just rough guesses; the mind converts them into certainty because it dislikes uncertainty.

A person behaving a certain way in one meeting does not mean that is who they are. A single expression does not define a personality. A moment of hesitation does not define courage. A moment of confidence does not define strength. A moment of silence does not define character.

People evolve when situations shift. Then, emotional states fluctuate. Finally, context changes everything.

But the human mind does not like this fluidity. It wants fixed definitions. It wants stable conclusions. It wants to turn uncertainty into something solid. So it takes probabilities and calls them facts.

This is where the selfie lens quietly locks into place.

Because the moment expectation attaches itself to perception, we stop observing and start predicting. And once we start predicting, we stop seeing what is actually there.

What we see now is what we expect.

And when reality does not match our expectations, we don't question the expectations. We question reality.

We call it unfair. We call it disappointing. We call it a mistake. We call it someone else's fault.

We rarely call it what it truly is, a mismatch between our inner blueprint and outer reality.

This is where most emotional pain is born.

Not because people are wrong. But because expectations were misplaced.

Not because life failed. But because imagination demanded control over something it never governed.

Not because relationships are broken. But because we expect them to heal something inside us that we have not yet learned to hold ourselves.

Once I started seeing expectation for what it truly is, something shifted quietly within me. I began to notice how often disappointment followed not reality, but imagination. How often irritation followed not behaviour, but unfulfilled prediction. How often hurt followed not intention, but expectation.

This awareness did not make me perfect. But it made me less blind.

And that was when I started to see others with a little more truth. It was also when I started being a little more honest with myself.

The moment I started paying more attention to expectations, I understood that it slips into every corner of our lives, not with announcement. But quietly. It doesn't arrive loudly. It arrives disguised as normal thinking. It feels harmless. Even practical. But it shapes what we notice and what we ignore. It defines what we amplify and what we dismiss. And slowly, without announcing itself, it becomes the ruler by which we measure the world.

I noticed how rarely I met situations without already leaning toward an outcome in my mind. Before a conversation even began, I had already decided how it would likely go. Before a person even spoke, I had already imagined the kind of response I would receive. I wasn't waiting for the world to show me what it was. I was quietly asking it to match what I had already prepared inside me.

And when it didn't match, my disappointment felt real. The frustration felt justified. The irritation felt personal.

It took me a long time to admit that what I was reacting to was not what was happening, but what I had expected to happen.

Once you see this, you start noticing how expectation quietly turns into projection. The moment we expect something from someone, we begin seeing signs of that expectation everywhere, even when those signs are not truly there. The mind becomes selective. It starts highlighting only the pieces that seem to confirm what it already believes.

If I expect someone to be careless, every small mistake becomes proof. If I expect someone to be warm, even a neutral gesture feels kind. If I expect someone to be unreliable, a single delay becomes a verdict. If I expect someone to judge me, even silence feels heavy with meaning.

Reality becomes secondary. Expectation becomes the narrator.

At that point, we are no longer observing life. We are editing it.

I began to understand how deeply this affects the way we relate to people. Many conflicts are not born from what was said or done, but from what was expected and did not arrive. Many wounds are not caused by actions, but by imagined obligations. We assume others know what we need. We assume they feel what we feel. We assume they should behave in alignment with our emotional state. And when they don't, we feel unseen.

But the truth is often simpler and harder at the same time. People are not living inside our emotional world. They are living inside theirs.

Each person is responding to their own inner weather. Their own fears. Their own distractions. Their own joys. Their own exhaustion. Their own private battles. They are not responding to our expectations. They are responding to their reality.

And yet, we judge them as if they failed us on purpose.

I saw this clearly when I began reflecting on how often I had expected understanding without offering explanation. How often I had expected support without expressing vulnerability. How often I had expected consistency in moments when even I was uncertain. How often I had expected emotional availability without checking whether the other person had the capacity at that time.

My disappointment, in many cases, was not because someone wronged me. It was because someone didn't live up to a story I never shared.

This is the quiet danger of expectation. It asks the world to read our minds. And when it doesn't, we call it betrayal.

I also began to see how expectations distort not just relationships, but the way we read strength and weakness in others. When we expect confidence, hesitation feels like incompetence. When we expect maturity, emotional fluctuation feels childish. When we expect stability, natural change feels unreliable. We forget that people don't grow in straight lines. They grow in pauses, failures, doubts, awkward transitions, and slow courage.

Expectations often overlook the process of growth and instead focus solely on results. As a result, they can be harsh critics.

I noticed how easily I would label someone based on one moment. One awkward reply. One quiet response. One emotional slip. And that label would quietly follow them in my mind long after the moment had passed. I would say I had moved on, but the expectation would still sit in the background, watching every future interaction through that same narrow window.

This is how the selfie lens gains strength. One assumption quietly becomes the reference point for all future perceptions.

And it doesn't stop with people. We do this with situations, with outcomes, with life itself. We wake up expecting the day to behave a certain way. We plan to expect the weather to cooperate. We work expecting effort to guarantee the result. We expect loyalty to return in the same form. We love expecting permanence. We try to expect clarity.

And when reality does what reality always does, move on its own terms, we feel either blessed or cheated.

We call it good luck. We call it fair. We call it bad luck. We call it unfairness. We call it someone else's mistake.

But beneath all those names sits the same source: expectation was placed where it never had control.

Nature does not respond to our plans. People do not unfold according to our hope. Life does not follow our mental timeline.

And yet, we keep expecting as if expectation has power over outcome.

This is what makes disappointment feel so personal. It feels like something was taken from us when, in fact, nothing was promised.

I once heard a line that stayed with me.

"Expectation is a contract you create in your mind and expect others to sign without knowing."

The longer I live, the more I see how true that is. We silently draw up emotional agreements with people who never agreed to them. And when those invisible agreements are broken, we feel wronged.

But how can someone break a promise they never made?

This is why expectation is not harmless. It builds emotional obligations that reality never accepted.

And when those obligations collapse, we confuse that collapse with failure.

We rarely question the expectation itself.

As I began noticing this pattern, I realised how deeply it connects to the idea that ninety-five percent of what we think we see in others is actually us. Our expectations come from our past. Our desires come from our unmet needs. Our fears come from our earlier wounds. And all of that gets projected outward as interpretation.

So when I judge someone as cold, I often discover that I am craving warmth. When I judge someone as careless, I often discover that I am seeking control. When I judge someone as inconsistent, I often discover that I am afraid of uncertainty. When I judge someone as distant, I often discover that I am afraid of being left out.

The other person becomes the screen. My inner world becomes the film.

And because the film feels real, I forget that it is still mine.

This is when the idea truly settled into me that we are not just seeing others through our past. We are also seeing them through our unmet expectations. And expectation is almost always tied to something unfinished inside us.

Once I saw that, I stopped feeling the need to be right all the time. I stopped needing my interpretation to win. I became more interested in asking myself where it was coming from. That shift did not make me passive. It made it clearer. It helped me separate what I felt from what was actually happening.

And the moment you begin to see that separation, the power of the selfie lens weakens a little.

Not because it disappears, but because it is no longer invisible.

You may still expect. You may still assume. You may still project.

But now you see yourself doing it.

And that changes everything.

Once I started noticing how expectation slips into perception, I began to see how deeply it shapes decisions. Not the loud, dramatic decisions that announce themselves. But the quiet ones that quietly redirect the course of a life. The people we choose to trust. The ones we keep at a distance. The opportunities we say yes to. The ones we avoid. The relationships we step into. The ones we walk away from too soon.

It is easy to believe we make these choices based on logic. But when I looked honestly at my own past, logic rarely arrived first. Feeling arrived first. Prediction arrived first. Comfort arrived first. And then logic entered later to defend the choice I had already made.

When I first entered the corporate world, I felt a strong sense of entitlement to a promotion, especially since I perceived my colleagues as not putting in much effort. By the end of my first year, I had gained a clearer understanding of my own capabilities and expected to be promoted. However, that didn't happen, and I was left feeling disappointed.

The following year, I was finally promoted and received a new title, but my salary increase was quite minimal compared to the standard for that position. Once again, my expectations fell short. Now, I find myself grappling with the challenge of managing these discrepancies between my aspirations and reality, reflecting on how the pressures of unmet expectations once felt overwhelming. Today, it seems like my expectations remain unfulfilled, but the burden feels different.

There were times I trusted someone quickly because something about them matched my internal image of safety. Their tone felt familiar. Their behaviour reminded me of someone who once made me feel secure. I did not know them well. But I felt confident I did. That confidence did not come from observation. It came from resemblance. And I called that resemblance "intuition."

There were also times I kept someone at a distance without ever giving them a real chance. Something about them unsettled me. Though I could not explain what. Later, when I traced that discomfort, I found older memories hiding underneath. An old hurt. An old betrayal. An old fear that had nothing to do with the person in front of me. Remember the girl I saw in college, or the first elephant I saw. The same things happened there, too. In all the cases, expectation guided the relationship long before reality had the chance.

This is how trust and mistrust often grow, not from knowledge, but from echoes.

The trouble with this is not that we make mistakes. Mistakes are human. The trouble is that we make mistakes with confidence. We label people before we know them. We doubt people before they reveal themselves. We attach meaning to behaviour that may not carry the meaning we assign. And once the label forms, it colours everything that comes after.

I have watched this happen in families. A child makes one mistake and slowly earns a reputation. Years later, even when the child changes, the old image still lingers in the eyes of those who formed it too early. Every new action is seen through the old conclusion. The label becomes heavier than the person.

I have seen it in workplaces too. A new employee struggles in the first few weeks and quietly gets marked as "not capable." Months later, even as the person grows and performs, the original assumption continues to whisper in the background. One early expectation shapes many later interpretations.

I have seen it in friendships, where one misunderstanding becomes a reference point for all future behaviour. Even kindness starts to look strategic. Even effort begins to feel forced. The past quietly edits the present.

All of this happens not because people are cruel, but because minds are fast.

The mind would rather be certain than curious. It would rather be right than open. It would rather hold onto a familiar conclusion than step into uncertainty.

Expectation gives it that certainty. Projection gives it that familiarity.

Together, they build a story that feels complete even when it is incomplete.

This is where the danger of the selfie lens becomes subtle. It does not trap us in obvious delusions. It traps us in convincing ones. It tells us we are reading reality when, in fact, we are reading our inner commentary. And because the commentary feels logical, we trust it.

I realised this most clearly when I began noticing how easily I could explain my judgments. Whenever I concluded something about someone, I could immediately list reasons. Their tone. Their timing. Their silence. Their body language. Their words. It all sounded neat and rational.

But the deeper I looked, the more I saw that those reasons were not causes. They were supporting actors. The main story was already written inside me before the evidence arrived.

I wasn't proving my conclusion. I was decorating it.

And that discovery unsettled me in a good way. It made me pause before speaking. It made me slow down before reacting. It made me question whether the certainty I felt was actually clarity or just comfort.

Comfort in being right. Comfort in being defended. Comfort in not having to stay unsure.

Uncertainty is uncomfortable. It asks us to wait. It asks us to observe. It asks us to gather more information. The mind dislikes that waiting. So it fills the silence with expectation and calls it understanding.

The older I grow, the more I see how much damage this habit quietly causes. People lose each other not through dramatic betrayals. They lose each other because of silent misunderstandings that never get clarified. Conversations end not because of truth. They end because of imagined meaning. Trust breaks not because of intention. It breaks because of the interpretation.

And all of it often begins with one small expectation that did not get examined.

I used to believe that being quick in judgment made me efficient. Now I see that it often made me inaccurate. It saved time, yes, but it cost depth. It offered speed, but it stole understanding.

There is a strange comfort in seeing someone as a fixed version of who they are. It makes the world feel predictable. But people are not static. They breathe, shift, learn, forget, heal, struggle, harden, soften. The moment we freeze them into one impression, we stop seeing their movement. And when we stop seeing their movement, we begin responding to an old photograph instead of a living person.

Expectation does that. It turns living people into still images.

Once I noticed this, something softened in the way I held my conclusions. I stopped gripping them so tightly. I gave them room to change. I began letting people surprise me again. And that surprised me, too, how much lighter it feels to not already "know" everything about someone.

It also changed the way I looked at my own mistakes. Earlier, when a decision went wrong, I would blame circumstances or people. Now I sometimes trace it back to the expectation that guided the choice. The prediction I trusted. The resemblance I confused for truth. The emotional shortcut I took.

That doesn't erase responsibility. It deepens it.

It makes me responsible not just for my actions, but for the unseen assumptions behind them.

And as that responsibility grew, the selfie lens began to lose its sharpness. Not because it vanished, but because awareness dulled its authority.

I still catch myself expecting. I still catch myself assuming. But now, I catch myself in the act.

And that pause, even when it's brief, is the space where better choices begin.

What has stayed with me through all of this is a simple and unsettling truth. Most of what I once thought I knew about others was actually a reflection of what was happening inside me. My expectations. My fears. My unmet needs. My old memories. My self-image. They were all quietly shaping my reading of the world.

I used to believe that disappointment meant someone had failed me. Now I often see that disappointment is what happens when reality refuses to cooperate with imagination. I used to think misunderstanding meant people were careless with words. Now I often see that misunderstanding begins when I read the intention without confirmation. I used to think conflict meant difference. Now I see how often conflict is born from unseen expectations colliding with lived reality.

None of this makes people innocent or perfect. It simply makes us human.

What changed was not the world outside me. What changed was how tightly I held my internal picture of how the world should behave. Slowly, almost without ceremony, expectation began to loosen its grip. Not because I stopped wanting things to go well. But because I stopped demanding that they unfold according to my mental script.

That shift didn't make life predictable. It made it more honest.

There is a quiet strength in letting go of the idea that the world owes us alignment with our inner blueprint. There is a calm that comes when we stop asking people to match the versions we created of them. There is a lightness in allowing others to be who they are. Even when that is inconvenient to our hopes.

When expectations blur, observation becomes more clear. And the moment you begin observing, your judgments soften on their own.

You listen longer. You assume less. You respond instead of reacting. You leave room for correction. You leave room for change.

And somewhere in that space, something deeply practical happens. Relationships become less heavy. Conversations feel less defensive. Decisions feel less rushed. Trust grows slowly instead of being forced quickly. Distance becomes easier to understand. And closeness becomes less conditional.

The most unexpected change, though, happened inside me. As my expectations of others softened, so did my expectations of myself. I was no longer demanding that I always be right, always be composed, always be emotionally consistent. I gave myself the same flexibility I had learned to give others. I allowed room for confusion. I allowed room for growth. I allowed room for not knowing.

And in that allowance, clarity began to arrive naturally.

There is a strange peace in recognising that we do not have to solve people in order to relate to them. We do not have to label others in order to understand them. We do not have to predict life in order to live it. We only have to stay present long enough to let the truth reveal itself in time.

The selfie lens does not disappear. It is part of being human. We will always see the world through ourselves. But when we become aware of that lens, it no longer controls us with the same force. It becomes a tool instead of a trap. It becomes a mirror instead of a verdict.

And that is the real shift.

Not the absence of projection. Not the absence of expectation. But the awareness that they are happening.

That awareness is what begins to clear the lens.

When the lens begins to clear, ninety-five percent starts to loosen its hold. The five percent of actual reality gets a little more space to breathe. People look less like symbols and more like individuals. Situations look less like threats and more like unfolding moments. Life looks less like a test and more like a movement.

This is not a dramatic transformation. It is a quiet one. You may not notice it immediately. But over time, it changes the texture of your inner world. Reactions grow slower. Emotions grow steadier. Interpretations grow kinder. Choices grow wiser.

And perhaps most importantly, you begin to feel less at war with the world.

You stop fighting people for not being who you expected them to be. You stop fighting situations for not obeying your plans. You stop fighting yourself for not always being certain.

You begin to walk with life instead of arguing with it.

That is where the selfie lens truly loses its dominance. Not when we try to destroy it, but when we stop letting it decide everything for us.

With that shift, the question quietly changes. It is no longer, "Why are people like this?" It becomes, "What inside me is being touched right now?" And that one question has the power to dissolve countless misunderstandings before they even take root.

This is where the journey moves next. Because once you begin to see how much of what you perceive in others is shaped by you, a different kind of curiosity arises. A curiosity about the emotional forces that colour your perception even further. A curiosity about the feelings that quietly tilt your lens without asking.

That is the next layer waiting to be seen.

Chapter 4: Emotions in Motion - The Hidden Filter

At first, I believed that judgments are incidental to thoughts. If one can understand their thoughts, they can understand their judgments as well. However, after much long, I realised that thoughts, more often than not, are late arrivals. Long before a thought appears, something else has already taken charge. That something is emotion.

At any given moment, whatever I am feeling feels like the truth. Not a version of truth. Not a possibility. The truth. If I feel hurt, that hurt is undeniable. If I feel anxious, the anxiety fills my body. If I feel calm, the world seems manageable. If I feel respected, I walk taller. If I feel ignored, something inside me contracts. These feelings are not imaginary. They are real experiences happening inside me. They deserve to be acknowledged.

In that sense, emotion never lies about me.

But I had to learn, slowly and sometimes painfully, that emotion often lies about others.

This distinction changed everything for me.

I did not make an effort to separate the inner truth from the outer reality for a long time. Every feeling was accompanied by the same assumption.

If I felt disrespected, I assumed someone had disrespected me.

If I felt judged, I assumed someone was judging me.

If I felt unsafe, I assumed something around me was dangerous.

The feeling was so convincing that I never thought to question the story attached to it.

Only later did I begin to notice a pattern. The same situation. The same person. Even the same words. But they could feel completely different on different days. On some days, a comment felt harmless. On other days, the same comment felt sharp. Nothing outside had changed. Something inside had.

That was when I began to see emotions not as windows to reality, but as filters moving across it.

Every emotion is born from a quiet collaboration between perception, memory, belief, and the present moment. Something happens. The senses collect information. Memory enters with past experiences. Belief assigns meaning. And the current situation provides the trigger. Out of this combination, emotion rises.

When it rises, it feels complete. Final. Self-evident.

The mind says, "This is how things are."

And in that moment, it truly feels that way.

But what I eventually understood was that emotion describes experience, not objectivity. It tells me how I am experiencing life right now, not necessarily what others are doing or intending.

If I feel disrespected, the feeling is real. My body tightens. My thoughts defend me. My emotions validate themselves. But the other person may not have intended disrespect at all. They may have been distracted. Overwhelmed. Preoccupied. Unaware. Even caring in their own way.

My emotion is real. The story I attach to it may not be.

This is where confusion begins. We turn an internal experience into an external accusation. Because the feeling is strong, we assume it must be accurate. But emotions are not neutral observers. They are shaped by memory. An old insult sharpens today's sensitivity. An earlier betrayal makes today's ambiguity feel threatening. The past quietly walks into the present and rearranges the furniture.

The moment stops being fresh.

I am no longer responding to what is. I am responding to what was.

This applies not only to negative emotions. Feeling good can be equally misleading. When I feel appreciated, I may assume respect where there is none. When my expectations are low, ordinary behaviour can feel extraordinary. When approval feeds the ego, warmth may feel deeper than it actually is. Again, the feeling is real. But it speaks about my need, not necessarily the other person's intention.

Understanding this did not make me emotionally distant. It made me emotionally accurate.

I stopped asking emotions to be judges. I started treating them as messengers.

They tell me where I am mentally. They do not tell me where others stand.

Once I placed emotions in their proper place, space opened up. Reaction slowed. Certainty softened. Curiosity replaced immediate conclusion. Compassion became possible, not as an effort, but as a natural response to clarity.

I learned to hold one sentence quietly inside me:

What I feel is real. But what I feel may not be the whole truth.

That sentence alone saved me from countless unnecessary conflicts.

I began to notice how the emotion dominating my mind at any moment became the lens through which I interpreted everything else. I rarely met people as they were; I met them as I was at that moment. My mood, my fatigue, my fear, my excitement, my dissatisfaction, my contentment, all of it quietly decided what I noticed, what I ignored, and what conclusions I drew.

The same person could appear warm one day and cold another, without changing at all. The same situation could feel manageable one moment and overwhelming the next. The external world stayed constant. The internal state kept moving.

Emotions do not stay contained. They spill. They colour the rest of the day. When stress takes over, the mind starts finding problems everywhere. When satisfaction is present, harmony seems easier to notice. When fear is active, threat appears where none exists. When excitement or overconfidence takes over, judgment loosens, and caution fades.

Fear, greed, joy, arrogance, anxiety, confidence, and dissatisfaction, none of these remain isolated. They explain the world to us.

And when emotions are strong, judgments become unreliable.

Because those judgments describe the observer, not the observed.

Fear and greed are not exceptions. Every emotion carries its own distortion. Euphoria can create overconfidence. Pride can blind us to feedback. Shame can make neutrality feel like rejection. Sadness can make indifference feel personal. Even calm can become complacency. No emotional state is neutral when it comes to judgment.

I saw this clearly in everyday life. When money was tight, conversations quietly revolved around possibility and usefulness. People became categories. When financial pressure eased, that entire way of seeing disappeared. Nothing outside changed. The lens did.

After watching a comedy, the world felt lighter. People seemed friendlier. Even strangers felt approachable. After watching a horror film, the same streets felt unsafe. Sounds felt suspicious. Shadows felt alive. The environment had not changed. The emotional filter had.

A fight at home could hijack an entire day. Anger or hurt would travel into work, into traffic, into conversations. Small remarks would irritate. Patience would shrink. On another day, without that emotional residue, the same person would appear calm, kind, and generous.

Which version was real?

If you consider it on an emotional level, both versions were real. But on an objective level, none of the versions is real.

That understanding was uncomfortable at first. It challenged the certainty I placed in my reactions. But it also freed me. Because if emotions are states, not truths, then they do not have to dictate my conclusions.

They can inform me. They do not have to control me.

This realisation was the beginning of a different relationship with my inner life. One where emotions were acknowledged, but not obeyed blindly. One where I could feel deeply without rushing to define others through that feeling.

And once that shift happened, something subtle but powerful appeared.

A gap.

A small pause between feeling and response.

That pause would change everything that followed.

That small gap I mentioned did not appear overnight. At first, it showed up only after damage had already been done. A sharp reply, I wished I had softened. A judgment I realised later was unfair. A reaction that made sense emotionally but created distance unnecessarily. Slowly, though, I began to recognise what was driving those moments. It was not logical. It was emotion in motion.

As I observed myself more closely, certain emotional patterns stood out again and again. Or, if we want to be honest, fear and greed in their many disguised forms.

Fear rarely announces itself clearly. It does not always feel like panic. Often, it feels like caution, seriousness, responsibility, or even intelligence. When fear is active, the mind becomes narrow. It stops exploring and starts protecting. It scans for threat, for rejection, for loss, for embarrassment, for uncertainty. And once it finds even a hint of these, it builds a story around them.

In a fearful state, neutral behaviour feels suspicious. Silence feels loaded. Delay feels intentional. Disagreement feels personal. The mind is no longer curious. It is defensive. It is not trying to understand. It is trying to survive.

I noticed this clearly in myself during moments of insecurity. When I doubted my own position, I became unusually sensitive to others' words. A simple question felt like criticism. A suggestion felt like control. Someone else's confidence felt like dominance. None of this was happening outside. It was happening inside me.

Fear does not change reality. It changes the interpretation.

And once interpretation changes, judgment follows naturally.

I realised that fear almost always pulls perception toward the negative. It exaggerates risk. It highlights worst-case possibilities. It treats uncertainty as danger. In that state, the mind does not ask, "What is actually happening?" It asks, "What could go wrong?"

And then it answers itself.

Fear also speeds up judgment. It hates waiting. Waiting feels unsafe. So it concludes quickly, even if the conclusion is inaccurate. Better to be wrong and protected than open and uncertain. That seems to be fear's logic.

This is why judgments formed under fear feel urgent and absolute. They carry a sense of "I must act now." And because they feel urgent, we rarely pause to examine them.

Greed works very differently, but it distorts perception just as strongly.

Greed does not always look like wanting more money. Often, it appears as emotional attachment, unchecked expectation, or the inability to tolerate uncertainty. When greed dominates, perception shifts toward usefulness. People are seen through the lens of benefit. Situations are evaluated by how well they serve our goals. Interactions become transactional, even if subtly so.

When greed is active, we notice what aligns with us and ignore what does not. We overvalue agreement. We overinterpret encouragement. We overlook warning signs. We hear what we want to hear.

I have seen this in myself during moments of strong hope. When I wanted something badly, I interpreted signals generously. Ambiguity became promise. Politeness became interest. Possibility became certainty. Hope filled the gaps that reality had not yet confirmed.

Just as fear narrows perception toward threat, greed narrows perception toward reward.

Both limit clarity.

Fear asks, "How can this hurt me?"

Greed asks, "How can this help me?"

Neither asks, "What is actually here?"

This is why decisions made under strong emotional charge often surprise us later. Once the emotion settles, the picture looks different. The person we trusted too quickly reveals the complexity we ignored. The person we feared reveals warmth we never allowed ourselves to see. The situation we rushed into or avoided now appears more nuanced.

The emotion moved on. The consequences remained.

This is when I began to understand something important. Emotional states do not just colour perception in the moment. They can shape long-term beliefs if we let them decide too much too quickly.

A fearful judgment repeated often enough becomes a belief about people.

A greed-based assumption repeated often enough becomes a pattern of attachment.

And once beliefs form, they continue shaping perception long after the original emotion has passed.

This is how temporary states become permanent conclusions.

I noticed this most clearly in something as ordinary as taste.

I do not enjoy curd even today, though many people love it. When I trace it back, there is no philosophical reason behind it. I was a toddler the first time I tasted it. On that particular day, the curd was not at its best. The taste felt unpleasant, and I threw up. That moment passed, but the emotional imprint did not. Years later, my body still reacts as if that single experience is the full truth about curd. The dislike feels instinctive, even though the original situation no longer exists.

I saw the same pattern repeat itself with my son. When he was around three, I gave him strawberries for the first time. Something about that moment did not land well for him. He disliked the taste and refused to eat them. Even now, though strawberries are objectively sweet and widely enjoyed, he avoids them completely. One early experience shaped a lasting conclusion.

What struck me was not the food itself, but the mechanism behind it. A brief emotional response, formed in a moment of discomfort, quietly turned into a permanent preference. The emotion moved on, but the conclusion stayed.

This is how emotions in motion leave traces. A single moment, especially when experienced early or intensely, can harden into belief. We stop tasting freshly. We stop checking again. The mind assumes that what once felt true must always be true.

The same process plays out far beyond food. An early rejection can become a lifelong sensitivity. One experience of embarrassment can turn into avoidance. A moment of fear can define how we approach similar situations years later. The original emotion may be gone, but its shadow continues to guide perception.

The same remains true with moods as well. In a low mood, people appeared indifferent. In a lighter mood, they appeared supportive. In anxiety, faces looked serious. In calm, the same faces looked neutral. In frustration, small inconveniences felt intentional. In contentment, they felt manageable.

This taught me something humbling. Emotional clarity is not about feeling less. It is about recognising what we are feeling before letting it explain the world for us.

Because once emotion becomes the narrator, facts take a back seat.

This awareness began changing how I handled difficult moments. Instead of asking immediately, "Why are they like this?" I began asking, "What state am I in right now?" That single question slowed everything down. It did not deny the feeling. It contextualised it.

I could feel angry without assuming someone was attacking me.

I could feel anxious without assuming something was wrong.

I could feel excited without assuming success was guaranteed.

That separation mattered.

It gave emotions dignity without giving them authority.

I also noticed how emotions travel. A stressful morning does not end at the front door. It enters conversations. It enters emails. It enters reactions. Others respond to that energy, not knowing its origin. And then their reactions confirm the emotional story already playing inside us.

A fight at home can make the world feel hostile. A good laugh can make strangers feel kind. A moment of shame can make every glance feel judgmental. A moment of pride can make ordinary acknowledgment feel like admiration.

The world responds, but not in the way we think. It responds to our emotional posture.

Once I saw this, responsibility shifted inward. Not as blame, but as awareness. If my emotions are shaping how I read the world, then managing them is not self-control in the moral sense. It is clarity in the practical sense.

I am not responsible for emotions arising.

I am responsible for what I let them define.

And this is where that gap between emotion and action became essential. That pause was no longer just a good idea. It was protection. For relationships. For decisions. For my own peace.

Because in that gap, fear could speak without ruling. Greed could arise without blinding. Emotion could move without hijacking perception.

That gap is where balance begins.

The distance between feeling and acting gradually turned out to be the most significant in my inner world. It was initially weak and unrealistic. Feelings would elevate, and responses would still spring forward. However, with time, as I started noticing the gap more frequently, it became stronger. It ceased being an accident and began to be a choice.

What surprised me was how much changes inside that small pause.

Emotion still arrives first. That does not change. A comment can still sting. A look can still unsettle. A delay can still trigger impatience. Fear can still tighten the chest. Greed can still lead the mind forward. The difference is not in what arises, but in what follows.

In the past, emotion would directly progress into judgment. It lingers now that I can take notice of it.

That silence does not fill the emotion. It allows it to breathe. And when a sentiment is given time to breathe, it tends to say more than it first purports to say. Under anger, there can be hurt. Under irritation, there can be fatigue. Under fear, there can be uncertainty. Under greed, there can be longing.

Once I see that, the story I was about to attach to the other person begins to loosen.

Earlier, I used to think that giving quick reactions was a sign of truthfulness and honesty. I thought that if I felt something strongly and I expressed it immediately, I was being authentic. However, in the due course of time, I understood that immediacy does not mean truth, not always, at least. Whatever is immediate could also be incomplete. But at times, delayed things have a chance to grow and mature.

This becomes more so when the emotions are strong.

The mind wants to shut down when it has fear in action. It wants distance. It wants control. It wants certainty. When I react instantly due to fear, I will tend to respond in self-defense almost every time. It will secure me, but it will also restrict my connection. It can make me safe in the short run, but it can frequently harm my knowledge in the long run.

When in a state of emotional attachment, the mind would wish to move rapidly. It wants to secure. It wants confirmation. It wants alignment. If I respond immediately from an emotionally charged state, my response will often be biased. I will hear encouragement where there is none. I will overlook discomfort. I will push past hesitation. I will move before clarity arrives.

In both cases, speed is the problem. Because emotions, when unexamined, rush us toward action. The pause interrupts the speed.

In that pause, I am able to ask myself simple questions. Not as a technique. But as a quiet check-in.

Is this feeling about what is happening right now, or about something older?

Is my reaction coming from fear of loss, or from the anticipation of gain?

Am I seeing the other person, or am I seeing what this moment reminds me of?

These questions do not demand answers immediately. Sometimes, just asking them is enough to slow the inner momentum.

I began noticing how differently conversations unfolded when I stayed within that gap. When I did not rush to label, the situation often clarified itself on its own. When I did not assume intention, people explained themselves naturally. When I did not react sharply, misunderstandings softened before they hardened into conflict.

What changed was not my ability to argue or defend myself. What changed was my willingness to wait before concluding.

This waiting is not passive. It is attentive. It is the kind of attention that watches the mind as much as it watches the situation. It notices when fear tries to take control. It notices when greed begins to distort. And in noticing, it creates distance.

That distance is not coldness. It is clarity.

I found this especially useful with people I knew well. With family and close friends, there is history. That history itself creates a natural pause. When someone close to me says something sharp, I already know their patterns, their struggles, their moods. I am less likely to freeze them into a single moment. I allow room for context because I have seen their complexity over time.

With strangers, however, the temptation to react is stronger. There is no stored understanding. There is no background to soften the moment. First impressions form quickly. Emotional responses try to take over. This is where the gap becomes even more important.

So, I understood that I need to be more observant and less interpretative with strangers. I did not determine who they were, but rather left them anonymous. I did not respond to a single behaviour but waited until I received more data. I remained inquisitive instead of making a conclusion.

Curiosity does something powerful. It keeps perception open.

I do not become hasty with assigning meaning when I am curious. I leave several interpretations to co-exist. A brief response may imply a lack of interest, or it may imply distraction. Serious tone may imply arrogance, or it may imply attention. Delay may connote negligence, or it may connote congestion.

Skepticism does not require certainty. It is comfortable with ambiguity. Reaction cannot remain comfortable like that.

I noticed that quick reactions led me to create a version of a person in my mind that was hard to forget. Even if the later realisations and evidence were different, the first judgement stayed. But when I stayed curious, my perception remained flexible. I could update it. Adjust it. Refine it.

This flexibility made relationships easier. Not perfect, but easier.

It reduced the weight of misunderstanding. It softened disagreements. It enabled room to be corrected without being humiliated. It helped to make conversations less of a confrontation and more of a dialogue.

It minimized regret most importantly.

I cannot tell how many times in the past I thought I should have paused before talking. Before deciding. Before reacting. That hesitation would never have taken away my feelings, but it would have spared my feelings the solidity of conclusions.

However, with time, I felt that life itself started reacting to being different when I worked out of this space. Not that the world was different, but that my emotional position changed. In situations that

I approached less urgently, they were not so threatening. As I became less assertive, people were less guarded. When I spoke with less assumption, people opened up more. When I listened without already knowing the answer, clarity arrived sooner.

This taught me something important about emotional intelligence. It is not about controlling emotions. It is about timing them. Allowing them to talk, but not allowing them to talk first.

Emotion has a rhythm. If we rush it, it overwhelms. Given a chance to settle, it informs.

And there is that little gap, that moment, the wisdom gets in.

It is not dramatic. It does not announce itself. It merely transforms the quality of our being. The presence, more than anything, is what makes us see other people.

When I am present, emotions still move. But they no longer hijack perception. They become part of the picture. Not the painter.

And that distinction makes all the difference.

With this increased understanding, I no longer viewed emotions as barriers to being clear. I started perceiving them as waves going through me. They came, lingered a little, and passed on. It was not necessary to prevent them, but to be aware when they attempted to grab the steering.

In the past, I thought that reality was characterized by emotions. When I felt something strongly, it must be true. Now I know that it is not facts that make experience; it is emotions. They write about the weather within me and not the landscape outside me.

It was a revelation that brought a good sort of peace.

I did not feel the need to struggle with my feelings and defend them. I could feel fear without assuming danger. I could feel greed without assuming benefit. I could feel hurt without assuming harm. I could feel joy without assuming permanence. Each feeling became a signal, not a verdict.

This shift softened the way I moved through the world. I stopped demanding that people match my emotional state. I stopped expecting situations to cooperate with my mood. I stopped assuming that what I felt must immediately be acted upon.

Instead, I learned to let emotions inform me quietly while I stayed grounded in observation.

This changed how I handled moments of fear. Fear still arose, but it no longer convinced me that everything was wrong. I recognised its protective instinct without letting it dominate my perception. Fear had narrowed the field of vision before; now I allowed myself to widen it again. I looked for context. I looked for alternatives. I looked for what I might be missing.

Greed softened, too. Wanting did not disappear, but it lost its urgency. I stopped rushing toward outcomes simply because they felt attractive in the moment. I allowed time to reveal what was aligned and what was not. Greed became quieter when it realised it no longer had to compete with patience.

And patience changed everything.

With patience, people revealed more of themselves. With patience, situations unfolded naturally. With patience, clarity arrived without force.

I began noticing how many conflicts in life are not about disagreement, but about timing. A reaction delivered too early. A judgment formed too quickly. A conclusion reached before enough information had arrived. Emotions rush us. Awareness slows us.

Slowing down did not make life dull. It made it accurate.

I also noticed something subtle but important. When I allowed myself this pause, others seemed to do the same around me. Conversations slowed. Defensiveness reduced. People felt less judged, even when disagreement existed. It was as if the emotional tone I carried invited a similar tone from others.

This reminded me that perception is not only inward-facing. It radiates outward. When I am calm, the world feels calmer. When I am tense, the world reflects tension back to me. Not because the world mirrors me intentionally, but because interactions are sensitive to emotional posture.

Once I saw this, responsibility felt less heavy and more empowering. I could not control others. I could not control situations. But I could choose how much of my emotional state I allowed to shape my interpretation of them.

That choice mattered.

Over time, this way of relating to emotions became natural. I no longer had to consciously remind myself to pause. The pause appeared on its own.

The gap widened. Reactions softened. Judgments loosened their grip.

Life did not become perfect. Misunderstandings still happened. Emotions still surged. Fear still whispered. Greed still leaned forward. But they no longer ran the show.

They became part of the movement, not the direction.

And that, perhaps, is the quiet power of emotional awareness. Not control. Not suppression. But recognition.

Recognition that emotions are honest about us, but incomplete about others.
Recognition that strong feelings do not require immediate conclusions.
Recognition that clarity grows when we allow time to pass through emotion.

As I look back now, I see how many judgments I once made were simply emotional snapshots taken mid-motion. Blurred images mistaken for facts. Freezing those moments into conclusions did not serve me or anyone else.

Learning to wait allowed the picture to come into focus.

This chapter completes another layer of the journey. First impressions, perception, projection, expectation, and now emotion.

Each one adds texture to how we see the world. Each one shows how much of what we experience is shaped internally.

The next step is inevitable. If emotions can colour perception so powerfully, then understanding how we carry emotions from the past into the present becomes essential. Because not all emotions are born in the moment. Some arrive carrying history.

That is where the journey moves next.

Chapter 5: The Social Mirror - Societal and Cultural Biases in Forming Perceptions

For a long time, I believed my judgments were personal. I used to think they came from my intelligence. I used to believe that my experiences drove them. I used to see them coming from my sense and perception of right and wrong. I used to assume that my reaction to someone or something was coming from me and was shaped by my thinking. But after years of understanding and a few uncomfortable realizations, I could see how incomplete my beliefs and thinking had been all along.

Society does not shape us through instruction. It shapes us through atmosphere. Through repetition. Through reward and discomfort. Through what is praised openly and what is ridiculed subtly. Through what feels safe to say and what feels risky to question. Over time, these signals sink so deeply into us that we stop noticing their presence. They begin to feel like common sense.

This is the social mirror.

We do not simply look at others and see them. We look at them through layers of social agreement. We look at them through the ideas that make things acceptable and respectable. We perceive them through our perception of what is normal and abnormal, successful and unsuccessful, appropriate and inappropriate, admirable or embarrassing. And we don't even tend to question them either. Why? Because these ideas and perceptions were absorbed early and reinforced often. We mistake familiarity for truth.

I began to take notice of it when I started paying attention to the speed with which my reactions would form. Someone would walk into a room, and before they would have scanned the room or even spoken a word, I would have made my decision of how that person might be and where they belonged. Not consciously. Not deliberately. But instinctively. Comfortable or uncomfortable. Impressive or ordinary. Trustworthy or questionable. Those judgments felt immediate and justified. Only later did I realise how little they had to do with the person standing there.

They had everything to do with what they reminded me of.

Clothing was one of the first places where this became obvious. We like to think we are beyond judging appearances, yet appearances often trigger our fastest conclusions. Clean, well-fitted clothes quietly signal discipline, seriousness, respectability. Certain styles feel responsible. Others feel careless. Some look "professional." Some look "out of place."

None of this is objective. But it feels natural.

When someone dresses outside the image we carry, a small shock passes through us. Surprise. Discomfort. Curiosity mixed with judgment. We may not say anything. We may even tell ourselves we are being open-minded. But something inside us has already reacted.

If we pause long enough, we may realise that the reaction is not to the person, but to a broken expectation. The person did not match the picture we were taught to trust.

Gender adds another layer to this mirror. Certain behaviours feel acceptable in one body. But they feel inappropriate in another. Assertiveness looks confident in some people. But it looks aggressive in others. Silence looks mature in some. But it looks weak in others. Emotional expression is praised in some. But it is discouraged in others.

We rarely ask ourselves where these reactions come from. They feel self-evident. But they are not. They are cultural habits that settled into us long before we could name them.

Culture itself works like invisible software. It runs quietly in the background, organising our reactions without asking for permission. What feels respectful in one culture feels cold in another. What feels affectionate here feels intrusive elsewhere. What feels normal in one place feels shocking somewhere else.

People carry their internal rules with them whenever they move outside their familiar environment. They continue seeing through the same lens. And that is even when the surroundings change. And then confusion arises when the reality is much different than that lens.

I noticed this clearly when I spent time with people whose backgrounds were different from mine. Behaviours I once took for granted suddenly felt ambiguous. Reactions I assumed were universal turned out to be deeply local. What I had always called "common sense" was often just "common where I grew up."

That realisation was unsettling. It meant that many of my judgments were not rooted in reality, but in repetition.

The inheritance of these lenses begins early. Long before we form opinions, we absorb emotional tone. Family becomes the first place where the world teaches us how it feels. Not through explanation, but through experience.

Before a child understands words, they understand safety, tension, warmth, and unpredictability. They learn what anger sounds like. What silence means. What affection feels like when it is consistent or conditional. These early experiences form an emotional blueprint.

If affection is steady, the child learns security. If anger dominates, the child learns caution. If emotions are dismissed, the child learns to hide. If mistakes are punished harshly, guilt arrives early and stays long.

These lessons do not announce themselves as lessons. They become default reactions. Later in life, similar situations activate the same emotional patterns automatically, even when the original context has long disappeared.

Community expands this blueprint. Community teaches emotional permission. It shows us which emotions are acceptable and which ones invite judgment. It teaches boys and girls differently. It teaches success loudly and failure quietly. It decides what deserves pride and what invites embarrassment.

At this stage, emotions stop being purely internal experiences. They become social signals. Pride becomes acceptable only when approved.

Fear becomes dangerous when visible. Belonging becomes conditional.

By the time school enters the picture, comparison begins to shape perception. Evaluation becomes normal. Praise and punishment link worth to performance. Curiosity slowly gives way to anxiety. Validation becomes external. Insecurity finds fertile ground.

Many of the emotions we later mistake as personality traits are learned responses from these environments. The quiet student. The competitive one. The people-pleaser. The rebel. These are not identities chosen freely. They are adaptations.

College intensifies this process. Exposure increases. Identity begins forming around emotion. Feeling uncertain becomes "I am uncertain." Feeling lost becomes "I am lost." Emotional intensity rises, but understanding often lags behind.

Then comes the workplace. Here, emotions are not welcome. They are managed. Stress is normalised. Fear hides behind professionalism. Validation shifts to titles, salaries, and authority. Old emotional patterns resurface in refined forms. Fear of authority. Need for approval. Sensitivity to rejection.

People are not reacting only to present roles. They are reacting to emotional memories that have followed them into new spaces.

Friends, too, play a powerful role. They reflect and reinforce beliefs. They normalise reactions. They validate judgments. Sometimes they offer safety. Sometimes they become echo chambers. Over time, group opinion quietly replaces personal inquiry.

And somewhere in this long process, something subtle happens. Borrowed opinions start feeling personal. Cultural habits start feeling logical. Group judgments start feeling insightful.

We stop asking where our reactions come from.

What makes this difficult to notice is that society rarely pressures us openly. It nudges. It rewards. It withdraws approval. It creates discomfort around deviation. The result is alignment without awareness.

We agree before we evaluate. We adopt before we question. We judge before we observe.

This chapter is not about rejecting society or culture. That would be unrealistic and unnecessary. Society is not the enemy. Culture is not a mistake. They provide structure, continuity, and belonging.

But when we are unaware of their influence, they quietly replace perception with habit.

The social mirror does not lie outright. It distorts by simplification. It turns individuals into symbols. It turns behaviour into categories. It replaces curiosity with recognition.

Learning to see that mirror is the first step toward seeing others more clearly.

And that awareness does not begin with changing opinions. It begins with noticing how many of them were never truly ours.

Once I began noticing how much of my perception was inherited, another question followed naturally. If these judgments were not entirely mine, why did they feel so convincing? Why did they feel so safe? Why did letting go of them feel unsettling, even when I could see their limitations?

The answer, I realised, lay in the quiet power of groups.

We are social long before we are rational. Long before we learn to think independently, we learn to belong. Belonging is not a preference. It is a survival instinct. Somewhere deep inside us sits the understanding that being aligned with the group once meant safety. Food. Protection. Acceptance. Being cast out meant danger.

That instinct did not disappear when society became modern. It only became subtler.

Today, alignment does not decide survival in obvious ways, but it still decides comfort. Approval. Ease. Emotional safety. When we agree with the group, life feels smoother. When we disagree, even silently, something tightens inside us. The discomfort is not intellectual. It is emotional.

This is why group opinion carries such quiet authority.

I noticed how often my certainty increased in the company. An idea that felt vague when I was alone suddenly felt solid when echoed by others. A mild suspicion turned into confidence after a few shared comments. A casual remark, repeated enough times, became a conclusion.

None of this required evidence. Repetition was enough.

Group opinion works by normalisation. When everyone around you reacts in a certain way, it begins to feel like the correct way to react. When a judgment is shared casually, without challenge, it stops feeling like a judgment at all. It starts feeling like an observation.

This is how bias hides.

I began noticing how often I formed opinions about people I had barely interacted with. Someone would be described as difficult, unreliable, arrogant, too ambitious, too quiet, or too emotional. By the time I met them, I was not meeting a person. I was meeting a reputation.

And reputations are powerful. They travel faster than reality. They shape perception before experience has a chance to speak.

I noticed something else, too. Even when my direct experience contradicted the group narrative, I hesitated to trust it. I told myself I must be missing something. After all, so many others felt the same way. Surely, they could not all be wrong.

This hesitation did not come from logic. It came from fear of standing alone.

Standing alone is not dramatic. It is quiet. It is the pause before agreeing. The silence after a judgment is made. The moment when everyone nods, and

you do not. That moment carries weight. It asks you to choose between accuracy and acceptance.

Most of the time, we choose acceptance without even noticing the choice.

I began seeing how much of my early agreement came from this place. I was not lying. I was aligning. I was allowing the group to do the thinking so I could stay comfortable inside it.

This does not make us weak. It makes us human.

But it also explains why first impressions become so distorted in group settings. Once a collective narrative forms, individual observation fades into the background. Even subtle differences get ironed out. Nuance disappears. Complexity becomes inconvenient.

The group prefers a simple story.

This is especially visible when someone does not fit neatly into existing categories. When behaviour is ambiguous. When personality is layered. When motives are unclear. Instead of staying with uncertainty, the group resolves it quickly by assigning a label.

That label then becomes the lens through which every future action is interpreted.

I saw this happen many times. A single awkward interaction becomes proof of incompetence. One emotional reaction becomes evidence of immaturity. One confident statement becomes arrogance. Once the story is set, every detail is recruited to support it.

What struck me was how rarely this process involved malice. People were not trying to harm. They were trying to make sense. But sense-making driven by comfort rather than curiosity leads to distortion.

Culture amplifies this effect.

Every culture carries its own unspoken rules. How to speak. How to disagree. How to dress. How much emotion is acceptable? How ambition should be displayed. How respect should look. When someone breaks these rules, the reaction is often swift and emotional.

Not because harm was done, but because expectation was violated.

I realised that many of my judgments were reactions to rule-breaking, not wrongdoing. Someone behaving differently unsettled me because it challenged the order I was used to. That discomfort quickly turned into judgment.

Once again, the reaction felt personal. It was anything but.

Social taboos deepen this effect. What is unspeakable in one society is ordinary in another. What is shameful here is celebrated elsewhere. When individuals move across these boundaries, they carry their internal rulebook with them. They expect others to follow rules they never agreed to.

When they don't, confusion turns into criticism.

I began noticing how often I expected people to behave according to my cultural grammar. When they didn't, I felt surprised, even offended. Only later did I realise that my expectation itself was the source of discomfort.

The person was simply being themselves.

This awareness shifted something important. It reminded me that discomfort does not always signal danger. Often, it signals unfamiliarity. And unfamiliarity is not a flaw. It is an invitation to observe more closely.

Group influence makes this observation difficult because it discourages staying unsure. Groups prefer conclusions. They prefer shared language. They prefer quick agreement. Uncertainty feels like hesitation. Hesitation feels like weakness.

But uncertainty is where truth often hides.

I noticed that the most honest impressions I formed came when I allowed myself to remain uncertain longer than I felt comfortable. When I resisted the urge to agree too quickly. When I delayed judgment, even when everyone else had already decided.

Those moments were not easy. They required emotional resilience. They required tolerating ambiguity. They required accepting that I might be wrong alone rather than wrong together.

Over time, I learned that wrong together still carries consequences. The group moves on. The label sticks. The person bears the cost. Shared error does not dissolve responsibility.

Seeing this made independent perception feel less like rebellion and more like integrity.

Integrity not in the moral sense, but in the perceptual sense. The willingness to see what is actually there, even when it complicates the social story.

This willingness did not isolate me. It grounded me.

I became slower to speak, but clearer when I did. I became less reactive to collective judgment. I became more attentive to my own direct experience. And slowly, that direct experience began carrying more weight than reputation.

That shift did not happen overnight. It happened in moments. In pauses. In quiet refusals to conclude too quickly.

Those moments added up.

And as they did, the social mirror began to lose some of its authority.

As I stayed with this awareness longer, I began to notice something more subtle and perhaps more influential than opinion itself. Society not only shapes what we think. It shapes what we feel, and when we feel it. And because feelings drive perception, the social mirror often enters our judgments long before any conscious thought appears.

The first emotion we feel toward someone often arrives as a sensation rather than a conclusion. Ease. Tension. Interest. Distance. Admiration. Discomfort. We rarely question these early sensations because they feel instinctive. We tell ourselves they are intuitive. But intuition, I was learning, is often just memory speaking quickly.

Those memories are not always personal. Many of them are social.

I noticed how certain accents immediately carried meaning in my mind. Certain ways of speaking felt educated. Others felt careless. Certain silences felt dignified. Others felt awkward. These meanings were not taught directly. They were absorbed over years of exposure to how people around me reacted. Laughter. Correction. Praise.

Ridicule. Over time, the emotion settled in before the thought.

By the time I noticed the reaction, it already felt justified.

This is how society teaches emotion without instruction. It rewards some expressions and discourages others until the body itself remembers what is acceptable. When we later meet someone new, the body reacts first. The mind explains later.

That explanation feels personal.

Its origin rarely is.

I also started to notice the shift in emotions as per the social context and surroundings. A person could feel approachable in one setting. But the same person could seem to be intimidating in some other setting. Someone's behaviour could seem confident in one place. But the same behaviour may seem inappropriate in some other place. The difference was not the individual. It was the social environment framing the interaction.

This framing is powerful because it operates invisibly. We rarely say, "I am reacting this way because of social conditioning." We say, "Something feels off." And because feelings feel real, we trust them.

I saw this clearly in myself during moments when I felt inexplicably cautious. There were people I hesitated around without any personal reason. When I traced that hesitation back, it often led to collective narratives. Stories I had heard. Warnings passed along. Generalisations spoken casually. Over time, these stories became emotional signals.

The emotion arrived first.

The reasoning followed.

I also noticed the opposite. Certain people inspired immediate trust, admiration, or respect before they had earned it. They fit an image I had learned to associate with competence or authority. Their confidence aligned with familiar signals. Their manner matched expectations. That alignment created comfort, and comfort created trust.

Later, when reality complicated that trust, I was slow to adjust. The initial emotion had already set the tone.

This is one of the quiet dangers of socially shaped emotion. It makes us overconfident in our first impressions. When an emotion feels socially validated, we rarely question it. We assume it must be accurate because it feels shared.

Groups reinforce this without effort. When others react similarly, the emotion feels confirmed. Agreement amplifies certainty. Disagreement feels unnecessary.

I realised that many of my emotional reactions were not responses to people, but responses to social signals carried by them. A role. A title. A background. A style. A perceived status. Once that signal was registered, emotion followed automatically.

The person underneath often arrived later, if at all.

This awareness made me gentler, but it also made me more alert. I began noticing when my reactions were too fast, too smooth, too familiar. Those reactions often had little to do with the present moment. They were echoes of what I had learned to feel.

I also noticed how strongly shame operates in this space. Shame is one of society's most effective tools. It does not shout. It whispers. It tells us what reactions are safe to express and which ones are dangerous. It shapes perception by limiting curiosity.

When a group quietly disapproves of someone, curiosity about that person feels risky. Asking questions feels like siding with the wrong side. Staying open feels like stepping out of line. Shame protects conformity.

I saw this play out when someone in a group became the subject of subtle criticism. Nothing overt. Just raised eyebrows. Shared jokes. A collective tone. Even when I felt uncertain about the judgment, I felt pressure to align emotionally. Not aligning felt uncomfortable.

This discomfort had nothing to do with the person being judged. It had everything to do with the group dynamic.

Recognising this did not immediately make me immune. But it gave me awareness. And awareness softened the automatic pull.

I began allowing myself to separate emotional response from emotional agreement. I could notice the group's reaction without absorbing it fully. I could acknowledge the shared mood without letting it decide my perception.

This required staying present. It required resisting the urge to resolve uncertainty quickly. It required trusting that clarity does not always arrive immediately.

What surprised me was how often clarity arrived later, when emotion had settled, and observation had time to accumulate. People revealed complexity. Situations revealed context. Early impressions loosened.

This taught me something essential. Many judgments feel urgent because emotion wants resolution. But resolution rushed through social conditioning is rarely accurate.

Allowing time felt like a small rebellion at first. Over time, it felt like maturity.

I stopped expecting myself to know immediately. I stopped demanding certainty from limited information. I allowed impressions to form gradually, through repeated observation rather than emotional reflex.

This did not distance me from society. It grounded me within it. I could participate without being consumed. I could listen without agreeing. I could belong without dissolving my perception into the group.

That balance felt rare and valuable.

It reminded me that society shapes us deeply. But it does not have to own us completely. It is not important for influence to become obedience. It is not necessary for conditioning to become destiny.

The moment we see how social emotion enters perception; we gain a little room to breathe.

And in that room, something quiet but powerful begins to happen.

We start seeing people again.

Once this understanding started to settle within me, I could stop looking at society as an external force acting upon me. Instead, I started to see it as an internal force living within me. A force shaping the way I interpreted the world. To me, society no longer remained outward in institutions, traditions, and norms. It started being inward, constantly present in my reactions, hesitations, comfort zones, and blind spots.

And this realization made me more attentive rather than cynical.

I noticed how often my reactions were rehearsed before the moment arrived. I would feel approval where approval was expected. Discomfort where discomfort was familiar. Pride where pride was rewarded. Embarrassment where embarrassment was learned. These reactions felt spontaneous, but they were anything but accidental. They were the result of long conditioning.

Once I saw this, the idea of forming an unbiased impression took on a new meaning. It was no longer about trying to be neutral or objective in some abstract way. It was about recognising when my perception was being guided by inherited scripts rather than lived experience.

Those scripts often appeared as quiet expectations. How someone should speak. How confident they should sound. How respectful they should appear. How ambitious they should be at a certain age. How calm or expressive they should remain in certain situations. When someone matched these expectations, I felt at ease. When they didn't, something in me tightened.

That tightening was the signal.

It told me that I was not seeing a person. I was seeing a deviation.

Deviation makes the conditioned mind uncomfortable. Not because it is wrong, but because it is unfamiliar. The mind prefers what it already knows. Familiarity feels safe. Unfamiliarity feels risky. Society reinforces this preference subtly but consistently.

I began noticing how this played out in everyday interactions. The way someone spoke could influence how seriously their ideas were taken. The way someone dressed could influence how much patience they were given. The way someone carried themselves could determine whether mistakes were forgiven or remembered.

None of this was fair. But it was real.

The more I noticed it, the more I realised how deeply unfair judgments were often unconscious. People were not deliberately dismissing others. They were responding to internalised signals that told them who deserved attention and who did not.

And then I noticed something harder to accept.

I was doing the same.

This was uncomfortable, but it was also liberating. Because if I could see my own participation in this process, I could also begin loosening its hold.

That loosening did not come from rejecting every instinctive reaction. It came from creating a pause around it. When I felt immediate approval or discomfort, I began asking myself what exactly

I was responding to. Was it the person in front of me, or the idea they represented? Was it their behaviour, or my expectation of how someone like them should behave?

Often, the answer surprised me.

I realised how many impressions I had formed without ever checking whether they were mine or borrowed. Once I began checking, many of those impressions lost their certainty. They became possibilities instead of conclusions.

That shift mattered.

It allowed people to exist beyond the narrow frames I had learned to use. It allowed conversations to unfold without premature judgment. It allowed relationships to develop without being constrained by early assumptions.

It also softened how I experienced difference. Earlier, difference often felt like disruption. Now it felt like information. Something to observe rather than resolve.

This did not make life slower in a frustrating way. It made it richer. More layered. More accurate.

I stopped rushing to decide who someone was. I allowed them to show me over time. I stopped assuming that my first reaction was insight. I treated it as data.

This approach did something unexpected. It reduced internal conflict. I no longer felt torn between what I felt and what I knew. I allowed both to exist without forcing them into agreement. Emotion could arise. Conditioning could surface. But neither had to dictate the final perception.

I also became more aware of how my own behaviour might be read through others' social mirrors. How I might trigger assumptions without intending to. How people might respond to what I represent rather than who I am. This awareness created patience. It reduced personalisation. It reminded me that misunderstanding often travels both ways.

Once you see the social mirror clearly, you stop taking reactions too personally. You understand that people are often responding to stories they carry, not to you directly. This understanding does not excuse harm, but it explains a great deal of confusion.

Over time, I noticed that when I stayed grounded in observation rather than alignment, something subtle shifted in my interactions. People felt less judged. Conversations felt less performative. Differences felt less threatening. Even disagreement felt cleaner.

This is not because I became neutral. It is because I became present.

Presence is the antidote to borrowed judgment.

When we are present, we do not need society to tell us what to see. We allow reality to show itself gradually. We trust time. We trust context. We trust that people are more than the labels attached to them.

This does not isolate us from society. It reconnects us to it in a healthier way. We remain part of the group without surrendering perception. We listen without absorbing blindly. We participate without disappearing.

That balance is delicate, but it is possible.

As I reflect on this chapter, I see it as an invitation rather than a conclusion. An invitation to notice where our impressions come from. To gently question which ones are inherited. To recognise that clarity grows not from certainty, but from attention.

The social mirror will always be there. Culture will continue shaping us. Groups will continue influencing us. That is not the problem.

The problem arises only when we stop seeing the mirror and start mistaking it for the world.

When we see it clearly, something shifts. Perception becomes lighter. Judgment becomes slower. Understanding deepens.

And in that space, we begin meeting people again. Not as symbols. Not as representatives. But as individuals, unfolding in real time.

That is where perception becomes humane.

And that is where the journey moves forward, into even deeper territory.

Chapter 6: Time and Transformation - The Evolution of Impressions

It was a long time before I realised that what we consider a first impression is actually not an impression. It is more like a reflex. A brief flash of recognition shaped by everything that came before the moment, but very little that belongs to the moment itself.

In that first encounter, I am rarely meeting the other person. I am meeting my own filters. My beliefs step forward first. My experiences speak before curiosity has time to arrive. My fears and expectations fill the silence quickly. The other person becomes a surface onto which my inner narratives are projected.

Time is missing from this exchange.

And without time, perception is thin.

At the beginning of any interaction, the mind wants speed. It wants to decide quickly. Friend or stranger. Safe or unsafe. Familiar or unfamiliar. Similar or different. These quick distinctions feel useful. They help us orient ourselves. They provide us with the feeling of control. Yet they tell us very little of the man we see before us.

They mostly tell us about ourselves.

I used to trust these early impressions deeply. They felt intuitive. They felt sharp. They felt intelligent. I believed that if something felt clear immediately, it must be true. Over the years, life quietly challenged that belief.

I began noticing how often my understanding of people shifted with time. People I once felt distant from grew close. People I once admired revealed complexity I had not seen. People I once misunderstood slowly became familiar in ways that surprised me. And sometimes, people I trusted early required re-evaluation later.

None of this meant I was wrong at the beginning. It meant I was incomplete.

Time was doing what immediacy never could.

Time introduced context. Time introduced a contradiction. Time introduced depth.

Without time, perception remains shallow. It stays on the surface, reacting to signals rather than understanding patterns. With time, perception begins to mature. It moves from reaction to recognition.

I noticed this clearly in relationships that unfolded slowly. At first, there were assumptions. I filled gaps with imagination. I interpreted tone through expectation. I assigned meaning where none had been confirmed. Over time, those interpretations either softened or dissolved. Not because I tried to correct them, but because reality kept offering new information.

Reality does not argue with our assumptions. It simply keeps living.

And if we stay long enough, we are forced to update our view.

This updating is uncomfortable. It challenges certainty. It unsettles the pride we attach to "knowing" people quickly. But it also brings relief. Because holding rigid impressions requires effort. It requires defending a story even when evidence changes.

Time makes defense exhausting.

I began seeing time as the silent architect of perception. It reshapes how we see without demanding attention. It works patiently, accumulating moments. A tone repeated. A behaviour seen across situations. A response under pressure. A reaction in ease. Slowly, a more accurate picture forms.

This picture is rarely dramatic. It does not arrive in a single revelation. It emerges gradually, like familiarity. And familiarity has a different quality than impression. It is softer. Less charged. Less certain, but more accurate.

I realised that when I allowed time into perception, my relationship with judgment changed. I became less eager to label. Less confident in early conclusions. Less invested in being right quickly. Instead, I became more interested in watching how people unfolded across different moments.

Time does not guarantee agreement or closeness. But it does guarantee clarity.

Clarity does not mean liking someone more. It means seeing them more honestly.

I also began to notice how unfair it is to freeze people in early impressions. We behave as though people are static, as though the image we formed once should remain valid forever. But nothing in life works that way. No moment repeats itself exactly. No experience is duplicated. Every encounter happens under different conditions, different moods, different histories.

The universe itself does not repeat. Why do we expect people to?

We accept change everywhere else. We accept that seasons shift. That circumstances evolve. That we ourselves are not the same person we were years ago. Yet we hold others hostage to versions we met briefly, often under incomplete conditions.

Time exposes this contradiction gently.

It serves to remind us that people are processes and not snapshots.

I could observe it easily with the help of looking back at my life. The individual I used to be when I was young does not exist anymore. My priorities have changed. My reactions have softened. My understanding has widened. Yet there are people who still respond to me as though I am frozen in an earlier version.

Their impression has not moved. But I have.

And I realised that I was doing so due to others.

This is where patience enters perception. Not as an ethical principle, but as a fact of utility. We never give perception time to play itself out, without being patient. We trap ourselves inside

the first decision point and refuse to move forward.

Judging someone too early is like entering a flowchart and refusing to move beyond the first box. Good or bad. Trustworthy or not. Similar or different. When we have a fixed way of thinking, we will not get out. The cycling of the mind is continuous, and it is supporting the same conclusion, not taking into consideration the new information that proves the opposite.

The loop feels safe. It feels consistent. It feels intelligent.

But it blocks growth.

Moving forward through that flowchart requires time. It requires allowing new information to enter. Contradictions to appear. Complexity to reveal itself. What appeared to be a form of weakness can prove to be a strength. What appeared arrogant could turn into insecurity. What felt distant may open into depth.

Time does not erase first impressions. It contextualises them.

It places them where they belong. At the beginning. Not at the end.

This understanding did not arrive suddenly. It came through repetition. Through being wrong gently, many times. Through seeing people surprise me. Through recognising how often certainty was premature.

Over time, I stopped asking myself whether my first impression was right. I started asking whether it was complete.

That question changed everything.

The longer I held on to this conception of time, the more I started realizing how unpleasant it is to have the mind wait. The mind prefers completion. It desires a story with an end, though the end may be imagined. Incomprehensible knowledge is perceived as a sign of weakness. Some certainty is like power. So we rush to close the gap.

Time, however, refuses to rush.

People tend to stand on the periphery of the unknown when we are first introduced to them. The mind responds to that strangeness by supplying blanks. It borrows from memory. It borrows from belief. It borrows from social patterns. It constructs a provisional version of the person and calls it understanding. This construction feels necessary at first. It helps us orient ourselves.

The trouble commences when we no longer regard it as provisional.

I realized that as soon as I became emotionally engaged with an initial impression, I ceased to observe. After making a decision about who someone was, I subconsciously started gathering evidence to back it up. Irrationalities felt annoying. Nuance felt inconvenient. I filtered experience through conclusion instead of allowing experience to shape the conclusion.

Time disrupts this habit naturally.

The more we interact with a person, the more they will act in a manner that does not match our perceived image. A person we thought was confident hesitates. Someone we thought was distant shows care. Someone we admired disappoints us. A person whom we disbelieve surprises us. These are minute aspects, but they do count.

All of them pose the same silent question: Will you change your perception, or will you justify it?

I have understood that perception can grow not as much based on intelligence, as it is based on the willingness. Willingness to revise.

Openness to admitting incompleteness. A moment of not outright rejecting something through judgment.

This willingness is only facilitated by time, not assured by time. It is possible to know someone for years and never see them because we are stuck to the initial tale, we have told ourselves.

This is where forbearance is more than patience. It becomes openness.

Openness is not passive. It requires attention. It involves observing trends and not exceptionalities. It involves observing the way a person reacts in various circumstances rather than a response to single incidents. Time provides the canvas. Attention paints the picture.

I began seeing how easily one moment can dominate perception when time is ignored. A bad day becomes a bad person. A quiet phase becomes indifference. A mistake becomes character. Without time, perception flattens everything into a single plane.

With time, layers appear.

I noticed this especially in moments when expectations collapsed. There were people I once admired quickly, only to feel disappointed later. That disappointment hurt not because the person had changed, but because my imagination had overreached. I had filled gaps with hope. Time slowly removed those fillings and revealed something more ordinary, more human.

At first, this felt like a loss. Later, it felt like realism.

There were also moments that went the other way. People I once felt unsure about gradually became familiar. Their silences began to make sense. Their boundaries felt less personal. Their rhythm became recognisable. What once felt distant began to feel steady.

Time did not make them different.

Time made them legible.

This legibility is what first impressions lack. They offer intensity without understanding. Clarity without context. Speed without depth. Time reverses that equation. It removes urgency and replaces it with familiarity.

Familiarity is often misunderstood. It is not closeness. It is not an attachment. It is simply recognition that grows from repeated exposure. It is the ability to anticipate without assuming. To understand without labelling. To see behaviour as part of a pattern rather than a verdict.

Patterns require time.

This is why judging someone early is like judging a book by a paragraph. You may sense tone. You may recognise the style. But you do not know the story. You do not know how it develops. You do not know what is essential and what is incidental.

Time allows us to distinguish between the two.

I also began to see how much pressure we place on early interactions. We expect clarity too soon. We expect comfort too quickly. We expect alignment immediately. When it does not arrive, we conclude something is wrong.

Often, nothing is wrong.

Time simply has not done its work yet.

We rarely allow this grace in modern life. Speed is praised. Efficiency is rewarded. Quick assessments are seen as a skill. But human understanding does not operate well under deadlines.

I noticed how much lighter my interactions became when I stopped demanding immediate coherence. When I allowed conversations to be awkward. When I accepted that connection does not always announce itself early. When I trusted that understanding unfolds, not appears.

This trust softened my expectations. It reduced the emotional charge around early impressions. I stopped asking myself whether I liked someone quickly. I started asking whether I was learning something new about them.

Learning requires time.

This shift also changed how I interpreted my own reactions. When I felt discomfort early on, I did not immediately treat it as a warning. I treated it as information. Something to observe rather than obey. Sometimes discomfort faded. Sometimes it clarified. Time helped distinguish intuition from projection.

Without time, those two feel identical.

Time does something else quietly. It reveals how much we ourselves change. The person observing is not static either. What we notice today may not be what we notice a year from now. Our sensitivities shift. Our priorities evolve. Our understanding deepens. The same behaviour can land differently as we grow.

This is why impressions are not only about the other person evolving. They are also about us evolving.

What once felt important may feel trivial later. What once felt threatening may feel neutral later. What once felt impressive may feel ordinary later.

Time matures perception in both directions.

I understood this most clearly when I looked at my relationship with my father.

When I was a child, my impression of him felt fixed and unquestionable. He appeared strict, distant, and authoritative. He worried about my behaviour, my studies, my discipline, and my time. In those years, I did not see concern; I saw control. I did not see care; I saw restriction. That impression felt complete at the time. It felt true.

But it was only partial.

As years passed, nothing dramatic announced itself. There was no single moment of transformation. No clear shift I could point to. Yet slowly, quietly, something changed. When I went to college, his way of relating to me softened. He listened more. He interfered less. Conversations replaced instructions.

At first, I thought he had changed.

Only later did I realise that we both had.

Time had been working in the background, reshaping roles, expectations, and understanding. The man had not suddenly become different; my capacity to see him had evolved. I had gathered more information. I had spoken to others. I had lived enough life to recognise patterns beyond my childhood lens.

When I became a father myself, the perception shifted again.

What once looked like rigidity revealed itself as responsibility. What once felt like distance showed up as concern expressed imperfectly. The same man, the same person, but a completely different understanding. Today, we speak more like friends. He is open to my ideas, less anxious about my choices, yet still quietly attentive, still checking in, still present.

The transformation did not happen in him alone. It happened in time. And it happened in me.

If I had frozen my perception of my father at the first stage, I would have missed the depth of the relationship entirely. Time did not erase my early impression; it contextualised it. It placed it where it belonged at the beginning of a story that was still unfolding.

I began seeing perception not as a judgment we make, but as a relationship that develops. It grows, shifts, refines. It is shaped by repeated encounters, by attention, by context, by our own inner movement.

When we allow this relationship to breathe, impressions lose their grip. They become starting points rather than conclusions.

And in that shift, something subtle but powerful happens. We stop treating people as answers and start treating them as unfolding stories.

That alone changes how we listen, how we respond, how we stay open.

What I began to understand, slowly and sometimes reluctantly, was that time not only adds information. It challenges belief. And belief does not like being challenged.

Beliefs want stability. The mind likes to remain there once it has made a decision. Alteration of a belief is like an acknowledgment of error, and the ego does not want to acknowledge this. It is due to this that once formed, impressions are difficult to change. They start out as observations, evolve into assumptions, and ultimately become beliefs.

Time threatens this settling.

Every new experience that contradicts an old impression creates tension. The mind can resolve that tension in two ways. It can adjust the belief, or it can dismiss the experience. Most of the time, dismissal is easier. It allows the belief to survive unchanged.

I noticed this pattern in myself. When someone behaved in a way that didn't fit my established view of them, my first response was rarely curiosity. It was an explanation. I told myself it was an exception. A mood. A one-off moment. Something not worth updating the larger picture for.

In this way, belief protected itself.

But time is patient. It keeps presenting new data. One contradiction is easy to ignore. Several are harder. Over time, the cost of maintaining the old belief begins to rise. It requires more justification. More mental gymnastics. More selective attention.

Eventually, something gives.

I also understood that most of the ingrained perceptions people hold are not necessarily true but rather hard to change. It disorients the internal order that we have constructed. It forces us to revisit conclusions we once felt confident about. It introduces uncertainty where certainty once lived.

Time introduces uncertainty gently, but consistently.

This is why people often say, "I don't know what changed." What changed was not the person alone. What changed was the accumulation of moments that could no longer be ignored. Time did not argue. It simply added weight.

I started perceiving belief as something that must not be fixed. Beliefs are helpful when they direct comprehension, and detrimental when they obstruct it. As the belief gets hardened, perception ceases to develop. We keep seeing the past version of someone even as they move forward.

This freeze is subtle. We may continue interacting, speaking, even caring. But we are relating to an image, not a living person. That image is anchored in a moment that no longer exists.

Time exposes this freeze by creating distance between the image and reality.

I noticed this very well in long-term relationships. On some occasions, I had even realised that I was responding to someone as to who they once were rather than what they became. My expectations lagged behind their growth. My assumptions were outdated.

That gap caused friction.

The same applies in reverse. Sometimes we underestimate people because our initial impression was narrow. We stop seeing their growth because it doesn't fit the story we began with. Time continues moving, but our perception remains parked.

This is where patience becomes transformative.

Patience allows perception to move with time rather than against it. It allows beliefs to stay provisional. It keeps conclusions open. It recognises that understanding is not a destination but a process.

I began practicing something simple, though not easy. When I noticed a strong reaction toward someone, I reminded myself that this reaction belonged to a specific moment. Not to the whole person. Not to their entire story. Just to what I was seeing right now.

That reminder softened the grip of certainty.

Over time, I noticed how much kinder this approach was, not only to others but to myself. I stopped demanding that I "get people right" immediately. I allowed myself to be in learning mode. Learning is lighter than judging. It carries less pressure.

Learning also aligns naturally with time.

Time is not interested in verdicts. It is interested in movement. It reveals how people respond to change, pressure, ease, failure, and success. These responses cannot be seen in a single encounter. They require duration.

This is why impressions formed without time are often dramatic but shallow. They are intense because they are untested. They feel meaningful because they are unchallenged.

Time tests everything.

I began seeing that the most accurate understanding of a person came not from how they appeared in ideal conditions, but from how they showed up across varied ones. How they handled disagreement. How they treated inconsistency. How they responded when things didn't go their way. These patterns reveal themselves slowly.

Time also reveals something else that first impressions hide. Context.

A behaviour without context is easy to misread. Silence can be an act of insensibility, and it can be numbness. Confidence can be arrogance, or it can be preparation. Distance can be indifference, or it can be self-protection. Without time, we assign meaning prematurely.

Time supplies the missing context.

It shows us what repeats and what was situational. It separates personality from circumstance. It helps us see what belongs to the person and what belongs to the moment.

I also realised that time not only softens negative impressions. It can also temper positive ones. Admiration formed too quickly often fades when reality introduces limits. This fading is not betrayal. It is a balance.

Balance is what time offers.

It replaces extremes with nuance. It replaces intensity with steadiness. It substitutes fantasy with familiarity. This may be disappointing initially, particularly when we are attached to the picture that we had created. But familiarity is not a loss. It is a more honest connection.

As this understanding grew, I stopped expecting people to confirm my early impressions. I allowed them to contradict me. I allowed myself to be wrong. Each correction felt less like failure and more like refinement.

Perception became something I updated, not defended.

This shift did not make relationships effortless. But it made them real. It allowed space for growth, for change, for misalignment and realignment. It removed the pressure of being seen correctly all the time.

And in that removal, something else appeared.

Trust.

Not blind trust in first impressions, but trust in the process of knowing. Trust that wisdom grows as time goes by. Trust that patience tells more than speed can tell.

And as I sit now with all this about me, what is most obvious to me is something I at one time had forgotten altogether. Time does not rush us toward truth. It invites us into it. And the invitation is quiet.

First impressions feel loud because they arrive without competition. They face no resistance. There is no history to correct them, no familiarity to soften them, no contradiction to challenge them. They appear whole, even when they are thin. That is why they feel convincing.

Time changes the rules of the conversation.

With time, impressions are no longer alone. They must share space with experience. They must answer to repetition. They must coexist with inconsistency. And in that shared space, many early conclusions lose their authority.

This is not because they were false. It is because they were partial.

I realised that much of the pain we experience in relationships comes from confusing partial understanding with final understanding. We expect people to remain loyal to versions we met briefly. We expect consistency where change is natural. We expect clarity before context has had time to form.

Time exposes these expectations gently, sometimes painfully.

When expectations collapse, it hurts. Not because the other person betrayed us, but because our imagination overreached. We mistook proximity for knowledge. We mistook intensity for insight. Time removes that confusion.

It shows us that knowing someone is not an event. It is a process.

This process cannot be hurried without distortion. It cannot be skipped without consequence. And it cannot be replaced by intuition alone, no matter how confident intuition feels.

I began seeing time as a teacher who does not explain. It demonstrates. It shows rather than tells. It gives a chance for patterns to emerge without comment. If we pay attention, we learn. If we rush, we miss.

Nothing can teach that more than time teaches people are dynamic. They are carved by time, strains, defeat, development, and transition. The individual that we are interacting with today is not the same as they were a year ago, and they will not be the same in the future. Holding anyone to a single impression ignores this movement.

We allow ourselves to evolve. We allow our views to mature. Yet we often deny that same evolution to others. Time corrects this imbalance.

It reminds us that perception must remain alive to stay accurate.

As this understanding deepened, my relationship with first impressions softened. I stopped treating them as judgments and started treating them as introductions. An introduction is not a conclusion. It is a beginning.

Beginnings are meant to open doors, not close them.

This shift changed how I listened. I listened with continuity, and not confirmation. I followed trends instead of instances. I observed the reaction of people when things took a new turn, when one was deprived of comfort, and when one got used to it.

With time, I was able to learn that maturity in perception is not a result of more acute judgment. It comes from restraint. From the ability to hold uncertainty without anxiety. From the willingness to let understanding arrive slowly.

This restraint is not passive. It is active patience.

Active patience means staying engaged without rushing to decide. It means being present without labelling. It means allowing people to surprise you without feeling threatened by the surprise.

In this space, impressions continue to form, but they remain flexible. They breathe. They update. They adapt. They are no longer rigid verdicts. They are working understandings.

And working understandings are kind.

They leave room for growth.

They leave room for error.

They leave room for change.

Time also teaches humility. It reminds us how often we were wrong. Not out of malice. But out of speed. It shows us that certainty formed too early is often the least reliable. The best perceptions are the ones that come in silently, when the urgency has worn off.

I do not question myself anymore about whether my initial impression was right. The assumption of that question is final.

Rather, I enquire whether my perception has continued to develop. Whether I am still observing. Whether I am still open.

Openness maintains the perception alive.

This does not imply blindly trusting and not taking precautions. Time does not remove discernment. It refines it. Discernment guided by time is calmer, steadier, and less reactive. It is informed by pattern, not impulse.

The myth of first impressions collapses naturally when we see this. First impressions are not lies. They are beginnings mistaken for endings. They are early sketches mistaken for finished portraits.

Time completes the picture.

And even then, the picture remains unfinished, because life keeps moving.

This understanding feels like a release. It removes the pressure to be right immediately. It removes the burden of fixing people into categories. It allows relationships to breathe.

When we allow time into perception, we give ourselves permission to learn rather than judge, to observe rather than conclude, to understand rather than assume.

In doing so, we do not lose clarity. We gain depth.

And depth, unlike certainty, does not collapse under change.

That is the quiet power of time. It does not argue with our impressions. It simply outgrows them.

Chapter 7: The Inner Work - How Can We Change Ourselves

Having taken so long to watch our impressions being made, how they are colored by our feelings, how we are all moulded by society, how time gradually rightens us, a question started to creep up in me. When perception continues to revert into the self, again and yet again, where exactly then does the change actually start?

The solution was embarrassing in its straightforwardness.

It starts with paying attention to myself. Not fixing myself. Not improving myself. Not becoming better than I am.

Just noticing.

For most of my life, I believed that change required effort in the outward direction. Reading more. Learning new techniques. Adopting better habits. Adjusting behavior consciously. These things have their place. But they do not touch the root. They operate on the surface. Where symptoms appear.

The deeper shift began only when I accepted something quietly obvious. I am already observing myself. All the time.

I notice when I am impatient. I notice when I exaggerate. I observe that I make judgments silently. I can feel that I'm faking listening. I observe myself when I am threatened, proud, insecure, and defensive.

The perception is already taking place. The one thing that is lacking is recognition.

In the majority of cases, I turn around and run away. I justify. I distract. I explain. I defend. I rush into the next thought. The observation passes through me without leaving a trace.

Change does not begin by creating awareness. Awareness already exists.

The first step to change is to be with it.

Something softened when I came to accept that I am the observer and the observed. I did not have to find any way to comprehend myself anymore. I simply needed to stop running from what I already saw.

This acceptance was not dramatic. It did not arrive as insight or clarity. It arrived as honesty.

I realised I was not blind to my behavior. I was unwilling to look at it without judgment. And judgment is exhausting. It either inflates the ego or collapses it. Neither state supports growth.

So the first shift was subtle. But it was also foundational. I stopped asking whether what I noticed was good or bad. I stopped trying to correct it immediately. I allowed myself to say, quietly, "This is what is happening."

That sentence changed everything.

"This is what is happening" carries no accusation. It carries no ambition. It carries no shame.

It simply opens a door.

From that door, the inner work begins naturally.

I noticed that observation without judgment leads to curiosity. That way, the mind does not become defensive. It does not push. It watches. And watching, over time, reveals more than force ever can.

This is where understanding others begins to shift.

Since I perceive myself in the same way that I perceive the world.

When I see myself harshly, I see others harshly. When I am in a hurry to make conclusions about myself, I am in a hurry to make conclusions about other people. When I tolerate complexity in myself, I tolerate complexity in others.

So the inner work is not separate from perception. It is perception, turned inward first.

Once this became clear, I stopped looking for dramatic changes. I began with the most ordinary moments of my day.

How do I wake up? Not what time. But with what mood?

Is there urgency before the day even begins? Is there resistance? Is it quiet?

I did not change anything. I just noticed.

How do I speak to the people closest to me? Not the words, but the tone underneath them. Is there patience? Is there irritation masked as efficiency? Is there affection mixed with expectation?

Again, no correction. Only observation.

How do I eat? Do I rush? Do I multitask? Do I finish meals without tasting them?

How do I drive? Is my body tense? Do I treat the road like a competition? Do I carry irritation into strangers' mistakes?

How do I consume information? What kind of content draws me in? What emotions does it leave behind? Agitation. Comparison. Desire. Fear.

How do I end my day? What thoughts occupy the space before sleep? Gratitude. Regret. Planning. Worry.

These observations did not feel spiritual or profound. They felt mundane. And that was exactly why they mattered.

Change does not begin in peak moments. It begins in repetition.

I started writing these observations down. Not because I wanted to remember them. But writing slowed my thinking. When I wrote, I could not escape myself as easily. The page did not argue. It did not comfort. It simply reflected.

Writing revealed patterns, I could not see in my head.

I noticed that the same emotions appeared at similar times. The same irritations surfaced in familiar situations. The same reactions were replicated with other people. Gradually, it came to light that it was habit rather than personality that I was dealing with.

This was not discouraging. It was liberating.

Assuming that habits determine identity, it follows that identity is not predetermined. When identity is not tied, then perception may vary.

This realization was not in the form of hope. It arrived as clarity.

I have realised that I have been expecting motivation to change. However, motivation is not reliable. It rises and falls. The familiarity with oneself is what actually helps in transformation.

In having knowledge of my patterns, I am less governed by them. Once I observe my reactions clearly, they are no longer urgent. Awareness comes naturally when I stop deluding myself that I am unaware.

From this place, something else appeared quietly. A desire.

Not the desire to be better than others. Not the desire to appear wise.

The desire to understand. To understand why I react the way I do. To understand why certain people trigger me. To understand why some situations confuse me repeatedly.

This desire did not feel heroic. It felt practical. It felt necessary.

And I noticed something important. This desire only arose after observation became honest. Before that, desire was entangled with ego. After that, it became clean.

The initial movement to change is a desire that can not be imposed. It manifests itself when awareness brings unease in the unconsciousness of living.

The course of the effort is important once desire has manifested.

I needed to examine why I needed to change my perception of people. Was it to control outcomes? To protect myself from hurt. To feel superior in understanding.

Or was it to live with less friction? To relate with less misunderstanding. To move through life with more ease.

This questioning did not need answers immediately. It needed sincerity.

Clarity of purpose does not arrive in a sentence. It settles gradually. And when it settles, effort aligns itself naturally. I stopped trying to change everything at once. I focused on consistency instead.

This is where discipline entered quietly.

Discipline is often misunderstood as force. For me, it became alignment. Doing small things regularly. Not because they were impressive. But because they were stabilizing.

Writing a few lines each day. Sitting silently for a few minutes without distraction. Noticing reactions before acting on them.

These acts were not spiritual practices. They were grounding practices.

Over time, dedication followed. Dedication is not intensity. It is continuity. Showing up even when there is no excitement. Especially when there is no excitement.

And when resistance appeared, as it always does, determination became necessary. Old beliefs surfaced. "This is unnecessary." "I already understand enough." "This is who I am." These voices were familiar. They had protected me once. They were not enemies.

Seeing them clearly reduced their power.

Slowly, something changed. I felt more centered. Less reactive. Less eager to conclude. My perception of others softened. Not because they changed. But because I did.

This is not a finish line. It is a way of living.

And it always begins the same way.

By noticing what is already happening inside you.

What surprised me most as this practice continued was how quickly resistance appeared. Not dramatic resistance. Not loud refusal. But a soft inner voice that said, "This is unnecessary," or "I already know this," or "I don't have time for this today." That voice did not argue. It distracted.

I began to see that resistance rarely comes as opposition. It comes as a postponement.

Tomorrow. Later. After things settle down.

But things rarely settle down. Life keeps moving. And the habit of not coming to know gradually turns to a habit of not wanting to know.

After realizing this, I ceased to struggle against resistance. Combating gave it strength. I instead made it another observation. I wrote about the desire to skip journaling when I felt like doing so. Where restlessness arose in silence, I observed the restlessness itself.

When it is observed, resistance loses its power.

This was an important shift. Earlier, I believed that discipline meant pushing through resistance. Now I began to understand that discipline meant staying present with it. Presence softened the struggle.

Journaling became central to this process. Not because writing is magical. But because it slows the mind down enough for honesty to surface. Thoughts that feel convincing in the head often sound exaggerated on paper. Patterns that hide in mental noise become visible when written consistently.

I did not journal about grand insights. I wrote about ordinary reactions.

I wrote about irritation in traffic. About impatience in conversations. About envy, I did not want to admit. About pride that disguised itself as confidence.

There was no audience. No performance. The page did not require consistency or coherence. It only reflected.

Over time, something subtle happened. I stopped being surprised by my own behavior. Familiarity replaced shock. And familiarity created space.

As soon as I am aware of my patterns, they do not have full control over me. They also still emerge, yet they are not urgent.

This is where the change of perception of other people started to become tangible.

Previously, in case someone annoyed me, I shifted out as fast as possible. I focused on their behavior. Their tone. Their timing. Their words. Now, there was a pause. I could see my own irritation forming before assigning blame.

That pause did not excuse behavior. It clarified the response.

I started paying attention to the fact that there were a lot of judgments, which were shortcuts made by an exhausted mind. A mind that is over with repetition, pressurized or unsettled emotion. The journaling allowed me to realize how frequently my responses were based not on what was happening in the present or what was happening to me, but rather the cumulative nature of fatigue.

This awareness did not require analysis. It required attention.

Another pattern became visible. My strongest judgments often appeared in familiar situations. The people closest to me triggered reactions more quickly than strangers. Expectations were higher. Disappointment arrived faster. The mind reacted to history rather than immediacy.

Writing about these moments revealed something humbling. I was often reacting to who someone used to be, not who they were right now. Old memories were speaking over the present reality.

Time had changed them. Time had changed me. But my perception had not caught up yet.

Seeing this softened my reactions. It made space for curiosity again.

Journaling also revealed how much of my inner dialogue was inherited. Certain phrases repeated themselves, almost word for word. Expectations sounded familiar. Criticism echoed voices I had heard long ago. The page exposed how rarely these thoughts were original.

This did not feel disappointing. It felt freeing.

If these thoughts were learned, they could be questioned. If they could be questioned, they did not have to rule perception.

Slowly, I began writing questions instead of conclusions.

Why does this bother me so much? What am I afraid of losing here? What expectation was violated? What story am I telling myself?

Questions do something important. They open the space. Conclusions close it.

As this questioning became natural, desire deepened. Not the desire to fix myself, but the desire to see clearly. To reduce unnecessary friction. To stop repeating the same misunderstandings with different people.

This desire did not burn loudly. It stayed steady.

With desire present, dedication became possible. Dedication is confused with intensity, which is short-lived. Dedication is quieter. The desire to go back, day after day, when nothing dramatic appears to take place, is the willingness.

There were days when journaling felt boring. Some days, silence felt restless. Some days, awareness felt heavy. Dedication did not require enjoying the process. It required staying with it.

Determination appeared when old habits pushed back. At some point, I felt like giving up the practice. Instances when clarity was disconcerting. When seeing myself clearly disrupted my self-image.

In those moments, I remembered something simple. I was not doing this to become perfect. I was doing this to become honest.

Honesty steadied determination.

Discipline followed naturally. Discipline was no longer about forcing behavior. It was about protecting space. Space to write. Space to sit quietly. Space to notice reactions before acting.

This space became sacred. Not because it was spiritual. But because it was rare.

Modern life does not offer much space for reflection. Without discipline, awareness dissolves into noise. With discipline, it stabilizes.

As these inner principles began working together, something else shifted. I felt less pulled by praise and blame. Compliments did not inflate me as much. Criticism did not collapse me as deeply. My center felt steadier.

From that center, perception changed.

People appeared less threatening. Situations felt less personal. Judgments slowed down.

I did not become passive. I became clearer.

I realised that understanding others does not require extraordinary insight. It requires self-stability. When I am not constantly reacting internally, I have the space to actually listen. To watch. To wait.

This waiting is not indifference. It is respect.

And in that respect, impressions mature naturally.

As journaling and observation became familiar, I noticed something quietly important. Awareness was no longer limited to the page or to moments of reflection. It began appearing in the middle of life itself. In conversations. In reactions. In pauses that had not existed before.

This was not because I tried to be mindful. It occurred due to the fact that the mind had been conditioned to slow down.

I realised that mindfulness is not a technique. It is a by-product. It comes out as a result of attention no longer being drawn out all the time. As the inner noise minimizes, consciousness enters the commonplace without struggling.

I observed it initially in minor responses.

Somebody would talk to me in a harsh tone, and instead of responding without delay, I would feel the constriction within myself. The need to react was present, but it was not so inevitable. There was a fraction of space. In that space, I could choose.

That choice did not come from control. It came from familiarity with myself.

I knew the pattern. I had seen it on paper. I had felt it many times. Recognition weakened its urgency. The feeling still came, but it did not hurry me.

This gap between stimulus and response started to be seen with increasing frequency. And with every occurrence that came, there was a change in perception. I could firstly observe the reaction within me as opposed to believing that the other individual had started my reaction.

That changed everything.

I ceased to perceive people as triggers and began to perceive them as reflections. Not philosophically, but practically. They demonstrated to me the location of my sensitivities. Where expectations hid. Where unresolved emotions waited quietly.

This did not make interactions self-centered. It made them honest.

I understood that disagreement is not the cause of many of the conflicts. They are about speed. Before comprehension sinks in, one response is received. Mindfulness makes the arrival slow enough that clarity comes in.

There was a role of silence that was not expected. Not silence as withdrawal, but silence as existence. Even taking a few minutes to do nothing without input or a distracter of any kind, trained my mind to remain with itself without experiencing uneasiness.

At first, this was difficult. The mind resisted stillness. Ideas flew by. Schemes were pictured. Memories replayed. But I did not engage with them. I noticed them.

Noticing without engagement changed the relationship with thought. Thoughts stopped feeling authoritative. They became movements passing through awareness rather than commands demanding obedience.

This shift mattered deeply for perception.

If thoughts are not commands, judgments are not final. If judgments are not final, impressions are not fixed.

I began seeing how quickly the mind labels. How effortlessly it categorises. It prefers certainty to curiosity. Mindfulness did not stop this process. It simply revealed it.

Once revealed, the process slowed on its own.

I also became aware of how often emotional residue from earlier moments shaped later interactions. A stressful meeting would bleed into the next conversation. An unresolved irritation would tint unrelated situations. Without awareness, these carryovers felt natural. With awareness, they became visible.

Seeing them reduced their power.

This awareness extended to the body as well. Tension in the shoulders. Tightness in the jaw. Shallow breathing. These physical cues often arrived before emotional reactions fully formed. The body knew before the mind concluded.

Listening to these signals allowed for earlier intervention. A breath. A pause. A moment of grounding. Nothing dramatic. Just enough to interrupt automatic reaction.

As this practice deepened, resistance changed shape. It no longer argued against awareness. Instead, it tried to co-opt it. I found myself in instances when I started to judge myself as being observant. Instances when consciousness became self-reproach.

This was an insidious and significant matter.

Consciousness hardens to a lack of pity. It makes surveillance out of observation. That was not the kind of space I would want to be in.

So I learned how to be kind by being mindful. Not indulgence. Not justification. Just gentleness. The recognition that patterns formed for reasons. That they once protected something. That change does not require punishment.

This gentleness allowed deeper honesty. I could look at less flattering parts of myself without collapsing. I could acknowledge bias without shame. I could see the limitation without defensiveness.

From this place, desire refined itself.

Earlier, the desire was to understand. Now, it was to remain aligned with that understanding. To live from clarity rather than impulse. To allow perception to stay fluid rather than rigid.

Dedication supported this refinement. Dedication meant returning to awareness even when life became busy. Even when stress increased. Even when old habits resurfaced.

Determination became quieter, too. It was no longer a dramatic resolve. It was simply staying. Not abandoning the practice when discomfort appeared. Not mistaking difficulty for failure.

Discipline continued to protect the essentials. A few minutes of writing. A few moments of silence. A conscious breath before responding. These small acts anchored the work.

Together, these inner principles created something stable. A center.

From this center, perception changed again.

I noticed that people's behaviors felt less personal. Criticism felt less threatening. Praise felt less intoxicating. Approval and disapproval passed through me without defining me.

This did not make me detached. It made me grounded.

When I was centered within myself, understanding others became simpler. Not easier, but clearer. I no longer needed them to behave a certain way for me to remain balanced. That alone removed a large source of distortion.

I could listen without preparing a defense. I could disagree without hostility. I could observe without urgency.

In that space, impressions matured naturally.

Understanding others did not come from analyzing them more deeply. It came from reacting to them less reflexively. The less noise inside me, the more clearly I could see.

This was perhaps the most surprising lesson of the inner work. Near-perfect understanding of others does not come from studying people. It comes from stabilizing oneself.

When inner chaos reduces, outer clarity increases.

As this practice settled into daily life, I began noticing a quiet shift in where I was standing internally. Earlier, I often felt pulled outward. Pulled by reactions. Pulled by opinions. Pulled by how others responded to me. Now, something felt more anchored.

I was beginning to experience what it meant to be centered.

Being centered does not mean being calm all the time. Emotions still arose. Frustration appeared. Disappointment visited. Joy came and went. But these emotions no longer displaced me. They moved through a space that felt stable rather than chaotic.

That stability did not come from effort. It came from familiarity with myself.

When I know my inner terrain, emotions lose their power to confuse perception. I can feel strongly without concluding blindly. I can be affected without being carried away. This difference made a difference in my relationships with people in a very practical manner.

Previously, when a person was very reactive, I had to respond according to his/her level. In case they were defensive, I was defensive. If they were cold, I withdrew. Assuming that they were violent, I stood on my feet. Their responses were reflexive and were influenced by their energy.

Now, I could stay where I was.

Being where I was did not imply disregard for them. It meant not abandoning myself in the interaction. I could listen without losing balance. I could respond without escalating. I could acknowledge without absorbing.

This is what centering offers. It creates a reference point that is internal rather than external.

From this reference point, old belief systems began revealing themselves more clearly. Beliefs about how people should behave. Beliefs about respect. Beliefs about success, failure, loyalty, and effort. Earlier, these beliefs operated silently. They dictated reactions without announcing themselves.

Now, I could see them forming.

When I felt irritation, I could often trace it to a belief being violated. Someone did not meet an expectation I had not consciously acknowledged. Someone acted outside a rule I carried quietly. The discomfort was not caused by their behavior alone. It was caused by the collision between reality and belief.

Seeing this changed the nature of discomfort. Instead of blaming outwardly, I became curious inwardly.

Where did this belief come from? When did I adopt it? Does it still serve me?

These questions did not require immediate answers. They loosened the grip of certainty.

Old beliefs resist change because they once provided structure. They helped us navigate earlier stages of life. Letting them go can feel like losing ground. But centering made this release gentler. I no longer felt like I was falling apart when a belief dissolved. I felt like I was making room.

This room allowed perception to breathe.

I noticed that when I was less attached to my beliefs, people appeared less threatening. Differences felt less personal. Disagreement felt less like rejection. This did not mean I agreed with everyone. It meant I did not need agreement to remain steady.

This steadiness changed the quality of my listening. I listened for understanding rather than confirmation. I listened without rehearsing responses. I listened without scanning for a threat.

And in that listening, something interesting happened. People often softened, too. Conversations slowed. Defensiveness reduced. Not always, but often enough to matter.

This was not because I was doing something clever. It was because I was no longer transmitting urgency.

Urgency fuels misunderstanding. Presence dissolves it.

Centering also changed how I related to time. Earlier, I wanted a quick resolution. Quick clarity. Quick reassurance. Now, I was more comfortable letting things unfold. I trusted that understanding would arrive when enough information was present.

This trust reduced anxiety. Anxiety thrives on premature closure. When closure is delayed intentionally, anxiety has less ground to stand on.

I also noticed that centering brought a quiet humility. I was less certain about my interpretations. Less invested in being right. More open to being corrected by experience.

This humility did not weaken perception. It refined it.

When I stopped defending my views aggressively, they became more accurate. When I stopped insisting on conclusions, clarity improved. When I allowed time and awareness to work together, understanding deepened naturally.

Old habits still appeared. Beliefs still surfaced. Conditioning still whispered. But they no longer commanded immediate action. They were heard, acknowledged, and sometimes set aside.

This is where discipline showed its quiet value again. Not discipline as control, but discipline as consistency. Returning to observation. Returning to journaling. Returning to silence. These practices kept the center intact.

Without them, the mind drifted. With them, it stayed grounded.

As this grounding deepened, the perceptions of others altered in a visible manner. I finally started to perceive people as processes instead of personalities. Their behavior made more sense when viewed across time. Their contradictions felt human rather than confusing.

I also became more patient with myself. I stopped expecting immediate mastery. I accepted that growth unfolds unevenly. Some days felt clear. Others felt reactive. Neither defined the whole journey.

This acceptance removed pressure.

And without pressure, change continued quietly.

As this centering became more familiar, I began to understand something that earlier felt abstract. Change does not arrive through force. It arrives through continuity. By lingering with oneself until old habits are deprived of their urgency and new visions are established.

Time, desire, and discipline began working together quietly.

Desire kept the direction alive. Not desire as ambition, but desire as sincerity. The simple wish to understand rather than assume. To relate rather than react. To live with less inner noise.

Discipline kept the ground steady. Without discipline, desire drifted. With discipline, desire found rhythm. The little everyday things were more significant than occasional intensity. Minor writing of a couple of lines when nothing entertaining occurred to me. Silence when restlessness prevailed. Taking a pause to give even what seemed to be an obvious answer.

These acts were not heroic. They were ordinary. And that ordinariness was their strength.

Time completed what effort alone could not.

Time softened edges. It allowed insights to settle. It let reactions replay themselves until familiarity replaced surprise. Over weeks and months, what once felt difficult became natural. What once required attention became a habit.

I observed that change was less transformative and more of a coming back when time had its way. I was not growing into a different person. I was shedding layers of automatic reaction that no longer served me.

This shedding was uneven. Some patterns loosened quickly. Others resisted longer. Certain judgments faded easily. Still others reappeared over and over. This would have been demotivating in the past. Now, it felt normal.

Growth is not linear. It spirals. The same figures are repeated again and again, with a bit less intensity, with a bit more consciousness. Every failure is not a failure of appearance. It is a chance to have a clearer sight.

I ceased to inquire about whether I had changed. I began observing my reactions that were not the same whenever I found myself in circumstances that previously distracted me.

Situations which would have been judged at once became open to inquiry. Things that in the past required a response could now be reflected on. Discussions that seemed to be threatening now seemed informative.

Such changes were not very noticeable, but progressive.

I also observed how this inner work exposed itself externally. There was a change in the way people reacted to me. Not that I tried to act in different ways, but because my internal condition was altered. People did not get as pressured when I was not as reactive. People were more open when I was not listening with an agenda. As I ceased to hurry in finishing up, conversations moved at their own speed.

This reflection was not manipulation. It was resonance.

The more peaceful the inner space, the more obvious the interaction on the outside.

I realised that I did not have to study psychology and the behavioural patterns to know others. It involves building up sufficient inner silence so that observation is made as a substitute for assumption. Expectations do not cloud the mind, and people portray themselves.

It is at this point that almost perfect knowledge starts to make sense. Not in the meaning of absolute accuracy, but with less distortion. Fewer projections. Fewer emotional overlays. Fewer borrowed judgments.

Perception becomes cleaner not because others change, but because the lens does.

I also became more forgiving of myself when perception failed. There were still moments of misjudgement. Moments of impatience. Moments of assumption. But these moments no longer defined me. They were seen, corrected, and integrated.

Correction did not come from guilt. It came from awareness.

This distinction mattered deeply.

Guilt freezes change. Awareness facilitates it.

As this awareness stabilized, a quiet confidence emerged. Not confidence in being right, but confidence in being present. I trusted myself to stay open. To revise understanding. To let impressions evolve.

This trust reduced fear. Fear of being wrong. Fear of being misled. Fear of losing control. When perception is flexible, fear has less hold.

I also noticed how this inner steadiness reduced the need to convince others. Earlier, disagreement felt like a threat. Now, it felt like a difference. I did not have to get people on my side as a way of preserving my perception.

This freedom did not keep me to myself. It brought me closer to reality.

I soon observed that the four inner principles, desire, dedication, determination, and discipline, were not things to accomplish in a sequence. They were qualities to cultivate continuously. They did not disappear once the change occurred. They sustained it.

Desire reminded me why I cared. Dedication kept me returning. Determination steadied me through resistance. Discipline protected the space for awareness.

Together, they formed a quiet structure that supported ongoing growth.

I also began trusting time more deeply. Earlier, I wanted results. Clear outcomes. Visible progress. Now, I trusted that time would reveal what needed to be seen if I remained attentive.

Time does not reward impatience. It responds to consistency.

This trust allowed me to relax into the process. I no longer chased understanding. I allowed it to arrive.

And as it arrived, perception continued to refine itself.

This is a journey that I continued, and something interesting became apparent to me. There was not a time when I could say, "Now I have finished." No starting line where knowledge remained in its place. Rather, it consisted of a silent transformation of my movement in life.

This interior work did not come to an end. It integrated.

I no longer considered awareness as something I practiced and began to experience it as something I carried. It manifested itself in my speech, my hearing, my hesitations, and my decision to remain silent instead of responding when remaining silent was more sincere.

This was no longer a discipline. It was alignment.

I also realized that I will no longer require reminders to monitor myself. Now observation was a natural thing, almost instinctive. Not absolute, not flawless, but accessible. In cases where I could slip into old habits, consciousness kicked me back into it. In this return, there was no punishment. Just recognition.

Recognition is enough.

With recognition, impressions changed shape. They no longer arrived at conclusions. They arrived as possibilities. A person was not immediately placed into a mental category. A situation was not immediately labeled. There was space for unfolding.

That space felt like freedom.

I realised that much of what we call misunderstanding comes from urgency. The urge to know quickly. The urge to decide. The urge to protect ourselves by concluding early. When that urgency softened, understanding had room to breathe.

Understanding others became simpler, not easier. Simpler because it no longer requires effortful interpretation. I did not need to figure people out. I needed to stay present long enough for them to reveal themselves.

Presence replaced analysis.

This presence also changed how I related to myself. Earlier, I judged my inner movements harshly. Now, I met them with curiosity. When irritation appeared, I did not condemn it. When insecurity surfaced, I did not hide it. I noticed, acknowledged, and allowed it to pass.

This gentleness deepened clarity.

Clarity does not grow in a hostile inner environment. It grows where honesty feels safe.

As time passed, I noticed something else. The desire to improve others' behavior faded. I no longer needed people to change for me to remain balanced. This did not mean I accepted harmful behavior. It meant I did not depend on others' responses to stay centered.

This independence felt light.

When you are not internally dependent on outcomes, perception sharpens. You see people as they are, not as you need them to be. You respond appropriately instead of reactively.

This is where near-perfect understanding quietly becomes possible.

Not perfect in the sense of complete knowledge. Perfect in the sense of minimal distortion. Fewer assumptions. Fewer projections. Fewer emotional overlays. What remains is a clearer encounter.

I also learned to trust time completely. There was no need to rush insight. No need to force change. If desire stayed alive and discipline remained gentle but steady, time did the rest.

Time revealed patterns. Time softened rigidity. Time corrected the misunderstanding.

I stopped trying to accelerate growth. I allowed it.

This allowance changed how I viewed the journey itself. Earlier, self-work felt like effort. Now, it felt like participation. Participation in my own unfolding.

There were days when awareness felt sharp. Days when it felt dull. Both were part of the rhythm. I ceased to gauge my progress by the degree of clearness that I experienced and began to gauge it by the degree of ease with which I regained my lost clarity.

Being back was not the same as being there.

It is here that bliss in its silent manifestation was starting to show itself. Not excitement. Not pleasure. But a subtle ease. The feeling that there was no longer the need to constantly interpret, defend, or control life.

People appeared less threatening. Situations felt less confusing. Even uncertainty felt manageable.

This did not mean life became simple. It meant it became honest.

And honesty is easier to carry than illusion.

As I reflect now, the inner work does not feel like a chapter separate from the rest of life. It feels like the foundation that supports everything else. How I see. How I listen. How I wait. How I change.

Understanding others became a natural extension of understanding myself. When I stopped fighting my own reactions, I stopped fighting reality. When I stopped rushing to conclude inwardly, I stopped rushing outwardly.

The world did not change.

I did.

And from that change, perception matured.

This is not a path reserved for a few. It is available to anyone willing to stay with themselves honestly. Anyone willing to observe without judgment. Anyone willing to let time do its quiet work.

The journey always begins in the same place. Not with others. Not with circumstances.

But with the simple willingness to see oneself clearly.

From there, everything else follows.

Chapter 8: Looking Into the Mirror with Awareness and Acceptance

There comes a phase in life when effort stops feeling scattered.

Until then, everything feels fragmented. Discipline exists, but without direction. Desire appears, but without clarity. Dedication appears but in spurts. We try different methods of work, different ideas, different philosophies, and hope that one of them will settle us down for once.

And for quite some time, nothing seems to work.

Years pass like this. Three, four, sometimes more. The same doubts return. The same questions circle back. Confusion feels familiar. On the surface, it appears to be stagnation. It is as if we are walking, but walking nowhere.

Yet under this apparent stagnancy, something is aligning.

All the inner forces slowly begin to face the same direction. Not through effort, but through repetition. Through living. Through failing quietly. Through understanding arriving too late and then arriving again. This alignment is subtle. It does not announce itself. It does not feel victorious.

And then, one normal day, light seems to shine.

Not the sort of clarity we were seeking. Not answers to the questions we kept asking. But clarity about the clarity we once believed we already had. It feels almost strange. The questions that once demanded resolution simply lose their weight. They do not get solved. They dissolve.

It is like stepping into a loop that does not trap the mind but frees it. A loop that keeps renewing insight without exhausting it. A loop that never seems finished, but never seems unfinished either.

I once heard a cricket commentator say of a batsman who had really settled at the crease: He said that when a batsman is in real form, he no longer sees a cricket ball. He sees a football. Large. Slow. Effortless to strike.

Nothing changes outside. The bowler is the same. The pitch is the same. The ball has not grown in size.

Only perception has shifted.

Life works in the same way.

When perception changes, effort reduces. Doubts soften. The ego, which once guarded every belief and reaction, starts dissolving without resistance. The inner world expands quietly. What once felt threatening now fits comfortably within it. Other people's egos stop feeling heavy. Their reactions stop feeling personal.

This shift does not feel like an achievement.

It feels like an upgrade.

I saw this very clearly through my child. He had problems with his eyesight when he was young. Objects appeared blurred. Details were incomplete. He had adapted to this world without knowing what clarity even meant.

When the doctor gave him some lenses, and he put them on for the first time, I was surprised at his reaction. He did not want to remove them. The world suddenly made sense. Shapes had edges. Distances had meaning. Faces had definition.

Nothing outside had changed. Yet everything had.

That is exactly how inner clarity arrives.

It feels like seeing life through an upgraded lens. What once required effort now feels obvious. What once felt confusing now feels simple. Not because reality changed, but because perception did.

This is where objectivity begins to feel different.

We tend to talk about objectivity as if it is fixed and universal. As if there is one right way of seeing things, and if you disagree, then someone must be wrong. But objectivity is not independent of perception. It is created by it.

When two people's objectivities align, we say they are "on the same page." When they do not, each lives in a self-defined world, convinced the other is mistaken.

The most difficult journey in life is not understanding others. It is stepping out of our own objectivity.

This journey takes years because objectivity protects identity. It justifies past choices. It validates beliefs. It offers certainty. And certainty feels safe. But safety comes at a cost. When objectivity hardens, understanding stops evolving.

When we finally step beyond it, the world does not become chaotic. It becomes independent. Free from our projections. Free from our expectations. Life begins to feel simpler, not because challenges disappear, but because resistance fades.

As an example, I often consider something as regular as a car.

At the most basic level, everyone doesn't argue with what a car is. A machine used to move people from one place to another. But the moment we get down to the deeper level, objectivity cracks. For one person, a car is about fuel efficiency. For another, it is status. For someone else, it is safety, comfort, speed, or brand image.

Each believes his or her definition to be closer to reality.

None of them is wrong.

Conflict does not arise from the car. It arises from certainty about perception.

This is how human disagreement is born. Not from reality, but from perception hardened into belief.

We cannot force ourselves into another person's perception. Nor can we expect others to adopt ours. Acceptance starts when we stop trying. When we look into the mirror, not to fix, correct, or improve, but just to acknowledge.

Accepting yourself in the mirror is not resignation. It is recognition.

At this stage, expectations begin revealing their true nature.

Expectations are not enemies. They give direction. They motivate effort. They fuel growth. But they also distort perception. They quietly demand that reality behave according to our inner blueprint. Until the expectations are clearly seen, the objectivity is still in a fog.

When expectations are softened, clarity is enhanced.

What we once demanded from the world, we now observe. What we used to fight against, we now know. The shift is subtle, but it changes everything.

This is where mindfulness starts to feel relevant, not as a practice, but a state. Ancient thinkers discussed whether the mind should be emptied or fully occupied. Perhaps the truth is in between the two. A mind that is alert and unattached. Active but unburdened.

In such a state, objectivity is no longer imposed. It reveals itself.

First impressions operate entirely inside expectation.

They arrive instantly. They are conditioned, remembered, believed, and feared. They appear convincing because they are uncontested. But they are not the truth. In this context, they are refrains of our inner lens at a particular time.

Time, in conjunction with awareness, melts away impressions. With clarity, impressions lose authority. What remains is understanding.

This is why first impressions are not long-lasting. Not because people change but because perception matures.

When the impressions are faded and expectations slackened, acceptance comes easily. We stop correcting others. We stop defending ourselves. We stop proving and protecting.

We simply see.

As acceptance started to set in, I realized something subtle, but important. Acceptance did not make me passive. It made me less defensive. There is a difference between the two, which I had not fully understood before.

In the past, whenever anything challenged me regarding my sense of self, I quickly reacted. I defended my position. I justified my behavior. I explained my intent. Even silence felt like a loss. Acceptance loosened this reflex. It allowed me to remain still when nothing needed fixing.

This stillness did not feel empty. It felt spacious.

In that space, empathy just seemed to come out. Not as a moral obligation, but because we see clearly. When I gave up battling my own imperfections, I gave up insisting on perfection from others. When I accept my inconsistencies, it makes me more tolerant of theirs.

Empathy did not come from imagining that I could be in someone else's place. It stemmed from the realization of how frequently I was confused, unsure, or incomplete.

This recognition made for a softening of judgment.

I realised that it is judgment that often hides discomfort. We make snap judgments because uncertainty disturbs us. Labels provide form to the unknown. They offer psychological relief. But they also close the door to understanding.

Acceptance does the opposite. It keeps the door open.

As I looked more honestly in the mirror, I saw contradictions, which I had ignored before. Strength together with insecurity. Confidence mixed with doubt. Generosity, followed by selfishness. These opposites did not cancel one another out. They coexisted.

Seeing something like this within myself changed the way I saw it in others. When someone was inconsistent in behavior, I no longer believed that they were being deceptive. I saw humanity. When someone contradicted him/herself, I did not rush to expose him/her. I noticed a familiar pattern.

People are not problems to be solved. They are processes that are unfolding.

This awareness shifted the tone of my inner dialogue. At an earlier stage, the mind was talking in conclusions. Now, it spoke in questions. Not interrogative questions, but open ones.

What might be happening here? What am I missing? What context am I not seeing yet?

Questions do not weaken perception. They strengthen it. They prevent premature closure.

I also noticed that acceptance took the need to compare. Where there is no acceptance, comparison thrives. When I stopped gauging myself against others, I stopped gauging others against my standards. Each individual began to emerge as a movement and not as a competitor.

This reduced envy. It reduced resentment. It reduced the quiet tension that comparison creates.

Acceptance also changed how I related to mistakes. Earlier, mistakes felt like exposures. Now, they felt like feedback. Information rather than indictment. This shift removed fear from learning.

But without fear, curiosity flourishes.

Often, curiosity is confused with interest. But true curiosity is an openness without agenda. It does not seek validation. It seeks clarity. When people were curious rather than judgmental, the interactions had a lighter tone. Conversations were explorative rather than evaluative.

I also saw how acceptance made me feel more at ease in terms of control in my relationship. Earlier, I wanted things to turn out the way I wanted. I wanted people to behave predictably. I wanted situations to make sense quickly. Acceptance loosened this grip.

I stopped trying to manage perception.

When control reduces, trust increases. Not blind trust, but trust in process. Trust that understanding will occur when given time. Believe that clarity comes when resistance is dissolved.

This trust was not only external, but also internal. I believed in myself to respond accordingly without rehearsing reactions. I trusted silence when words felt unnecessary. I trusted pauses without filling them.

These pauses became powerful.

In those pauses, there was even more empathy. I could hear not only what was said, but what was not said. Not only words, but hesitations. Not just reactions, but the emotional roots of them.

Empathy didn't make me agree with anyone and everything. It gave me the opportunity to be able to understand disagreement without hostility.

The natural response to this was compassion.

Compassion is generally misinterpreted as softness. In reality, it is strength but not rigidity. It views suffering but does not dramatize it. It recognises limitation without despising it.

When I took a look at others through this lens, behavior that previously irritated me showed vulnerability. Defensiveness revealed fear. Arrogance revealed insecurity. Silence revealed overwhelm. None of these justified harmful actions, but they contextualised them.

Context does not excuse behavior. It clarifies it.

This clarity allowed conviction to form. Conviction not in judging others, but in knowing when and how to respond. Acceptance did not dissolve boundaries. It made them cleaner.

Earlier, boundaries were reactive. Now, they felt intentional.

I could say no without anger. I could disagree without attack. I could withdraw without resentment.

This balance was due to self-acceptance.

When we cease to fight ourselves, we cease to fight the world.

The mirror no longer reflected flaws that required correction. It reflected patterns that needed understanding. And understanding changed the way I was standing in relationship to others.

I did not have to prove my perception was correct anymore. I allowed it to evolve. I did not attach myself to first impressions. I allowed second, third, and fourth impressions to modify them.

This flexibility did not weaken conviction. It refined it.

Conviction built on acceptance is calm. It does not shout. It does not rush. It waits until clarity feels settled before acting.

This is where reflective living replaced reactive living.

Reaction demands immediacy. Reflection calls for patience.

Reflection does not deny emotion. It places it correctly. It allows feeling without surrendering to it. It listens without concluding.

As this reflective approach settled in, I realised that accuracy in judgment does not come from sharpness. It comes from stillness. From allowing enough space for reality to speak.

Acceptance creates that space.

As acceptance had settled more deeply, I started seeing how much internal resistance had been shaping my perception without my awareness. Resistance is subtle. It does not always appear as opposition. Often, it shows up as insistence. Insistence that things should be different. That people should know better. That situations should resolve faster.

Resistance is the refusal to accept reality where it is.

In my earlier experiences, I misinterpreted resistance as discernment. I believed that holding firm opinions meant clarity. Now I began seeing how often those opinions were built on discomfort rather than understanding. Resistance was not protecting the truth. It was protecting familiarity.

Familiarity is safe, even when it is limiting.

I noticed that whenever I felt contracted internally, the perception narrowed. My view became selective. I gave attention to what confirmed what I expected and blocked out what contradicted my expectations. This constriction felt like certainty but was actually avoidance.

Acceptance increased perception.

When I gave up fighting what I felt, what others expressed, and what situations presented, this field of awareness expanded. I was able to hold conflicting information without having to rush to resolve it. I could allow ambiguity without anxiety.

Ambiguity stopped feeling like a threat.

This shift changed how expectations functioned within me. Earlier, expectations felt necessary. They gave structure. They offered direction. They helped me plan and predict. But I began noticing how expectations quietly demanded compliance from reality.

When reality complied, I felt validated. When it didn't, I felt wronged.

Acceptance softened this dynamic.

Expectations did not disappear. They became visible. Once visible, they lost authority. I could see when disappointment arose not from harm, but from unmet assumptions. I could separate inconvenience from injustice. Difference from disrespect.

This clarity reduced emotional charge.

I also realised how often resistance came from unresolved inner conflict. Parts of me wanted change. Other parts wanted stability. Acceptance did not choose sides. It acknowledged both.

This acknowledgment reduced inner friction.

When inner conflict reduced, perception became cleaner. I was no longer putting my own tension on others. I was no longer demanding that they solve what I was not yet reconciled with within my own self.

This was liberating.

I began seeing how much of interpersonal conflict originates from intrapersonal resistance. We react outwardly to avoid meeting something inwardly. Acceptance interrupts this transfer.

As resistance dissolved, reflection deepened.

Reflection is not analysis. It is presence with awareness. It does not dissect experience. It allows experience to reveal itself. When I reflected rather than reacted, responses emerged organically.

This organic response felt appropriate rather than clever.

I also noticed how acceptance changed my relationship with silence. Earlier, silence felt awkward. It demanded filling. Now, silence felt informative. It carried texture. It allowed things to settle.

In silence, expectations loosened further. I did not need immediate coherence. I allowed meaning to arrive slowly.

This slow arrival changed the quality of insight.

Insight no longer felt like discovery. It felt like recognition.

Recognition is gentler than revelation. It does not shock the system. It integrates smoothly. Acceptance prepares the ground for recognition.

As this recognition deepened, I noticed how little energy was spent defending identity. Earlier, identity felt fragile. It was necessary for constant reinforcement. Opinions, beliefs, and reactions were used for scaffolding.

Acceptance eliminated the need for scaffolding.

When there is no threat to identity, perception becomes relaxed. We are not scanning for validation or rejection. We are not filtering experience through self-protection. We are simply present.

Presence changed how I interpreted others' behavior.

I stopped asking what their behavior meant about me. I started seeing what it revealed about their state, their conditioning, their moment. This shift reduced personalization.

Personalization fuels misunderstanding. De-personalization invites clarity.

This did not make interactions cold. It made them accurate.

I also noticed how acceptance allowed compassion without entanglement. I could care without absorbing. I could empathize without losing boundaries. Compassion did not mean agreeing. It meant understanding context.

Context softened judgment without dissolving discernment.

Earlier, discernment felt sharp and defensive. Now, it felt grounded and patient. I did not have to respond to every inconsistency. I could watch patterns unfold.

Patterns require time and acceptance.

Acceptance allowed me to remain open long enough to see patterns rather than fragments. Fragments invite judgment. Patterns invite understanding.

This shift was subtle, but profound.

I also noticed that acceptance did not get rid of emotional reactions. It changed their lifespan. Emotions arose, but they were passing faster. They did not linger as stories. They did not harden into beliefs.

This transience created freedom.

Freedom does not mean absence of emotion. It means the absence of attachment to emotion as truth.

As the acceptance deepened, my inner dialogue became softer. The tone changed. It became less accusatory. Less demanding. More curious. This tone carried outward naturally.

People responded differently. Conversations slowed. Defensiveness reduced. Not always, but enough to notice.

Acceptance sends a message of safety.

When others perceive that they are safe, they open up more. The more they reveal, the greater the understanding. Read from here

This is how accurate judgment forms. Not from sharp intellect, but from a safe inner environment.

I also began noticing how acceptance changed my relationship with failure. Failure lost its sting. It became information. I could look at mistakes without shrinking. This resilience allowed perception to remain open even when things went wrong.

Closed perception seeks blame. Open perception seeks learning.

Acceptance supports the latter.

As this reflective approach became more mature, I wasn't as in a rush to draw conclusions. I trusted that understanding would come if I were present. This trust reduced anxiety.

Anxiety thrives on premature closure. Acceptance delays closure until clarity feels natural.

This delay is not avoidance. It is wisdom.

In this space, looking into the mirror felt different. The mirror no longer reflected flaws demanding correction. It reflected movement. Growth. Imperfection without judgment.

This reflection fostered humility. Not self-doubt. But realism. The understanding that perception is always partial. Always evolving.

Humility kept perception flexible.

And flexibility allowed compassion to remain alive.

As acceptance settled more firmly, I noticed how differently I began to experience relationships. Earlier, relationships had the feel of negotiations. There was an unspoken effort to be understood, to be valued, to be met in a certain way. Even affection carried expectations. Even closeness carried demands.

Acceptance loosened this tension.

I no longer went into interactions with a checklist in silence as to how things should unfold. Conversations became less about coming to an agreement and more about finding perspective. I was no longer trying to make people fit my inner narrative. I was letting their story speak for itself.

This altered the feel of disagreement.

In the past, disagreement was personal. It was rejection, dismissal; it felt like rejection. I reacted to not the idea itself, but what I thought it said about me. Acceptance was able to remove that layer. Once the issue of identity is no longer at stake, disagreement is information and not a threat.

I was able to listen and not prepare a counterpoint. I could disagree without tightening inside. I could express my view without insisting on dominance.

This was not indifference. It was clarity.

Conviction still existed. In fact, it became stronger. But it was no longer rigid. It did not need reinforcement. Conviction grounded in acceptance does not shout. It does not rush to prove itself. It rests comfortably in uncertainty.

Earlier, conviction was something I defended. Now, it was something I carried lightly.

This lightness made conversations more honest. I noticed that when I was not pushing my perspective, others felt less defensive. When being defensive decreased, real dialogue became possible. Not agreement, but exchange.

Exchange is more substantial than consensus.

I also noticed the change in my interpretation of emotional reaction in others, as acceptance changed the way I interpreted emotional reaction. Earlier, strong emotions caused either resistance or withdrawal in me. Now, they stimulated curiosity. I started to recognize emotion as information about the other person's inner state, and not something that is a weapon against me.

This shift reduced conflict significantly.

Conflict thrives on misinterpretation. Acceptance corrects interpretation.

I did not have to absorb the feelings of others to acknowledge them. I was able to recognize distress without being destabilized by it. This balance enabled me to be present even in challenging conversations.

Presence itself became the greatest contribution that I could offer.

I also saw acceptance change compassion. At an earlier time, feeling compassion was an effort. It required being reminded to be kind. Now, it felt automatic. When judgment loosened, compassion took its natural place in it.

Compassion did not involve being agreeable with harmful behavior. It meant understanding the conditions that created it. This understanding did not excuse harm. It contextualised it.

Context prevents dehumanization.

I began seeing how quickly we reduce people to moments. A single reaction. A single mistake. A single disagreement. Acceptance refused to freeze people in these moments. It insisted on continuity. On remembering that no one is fully represented by a fragment.

This insistence softened my internal language. I stopped describing people as problems. I stopped defining them by behavior alone. I saw them as complex systems responding to pressures I could not fully see.

This perspective changed how I set boundaries. Boundaries no longer came from resentment. They came from clarity. I could step back without anger. I could say no without explanation. I could disengage without punishment.

Boundaries guided by acceptance are clean.

Earlier, boundaries were reactive. They carried emotional residue. Now, they felt neutral. Necessary but not hostile.

I also noticed I was changing the way I handled being misunderstood because of acceptance. Earlier misunderstandings had felt intolerable. I wanted to make myself clear straight away. To correct perception. To restore alignment.

Now, I was able to tolerate being misunderstood. Not indefinitely, but without panic. I trusted that time and consistency would correct what explanation could not.

This trust reduced urgency.

Urgency is mistakenly considered to be sincerity.

Calm is often confused with indifference.

Acceptance helped me not to lose my cool by disconnecting.

I also saw how acceptance transformed my relationship to approval. Earlier, approval had a validating feeling. Disapproval felt diminishing. Now, both felt informational. Neither defined me.

This independence did not isolate me. It freed me.

When we are not dependent on approbation, we are free to see others accurately. We are not distorting perception for the benefit of self-image. We are not distorting reality to maintain belonging.

This freedom sharpened discernment.

Discernment guided by acceptance is patient. It does not rush to label. It waits for patterns. It watches consistency across time. It distinguishes between mood and character, reaction and pattern.

Patterns reveal truth.

Acceptance enabled me to be there long enough to see those patterns. Earlier, discomfort would drive me away too quickly. Now, I could be present without taking in negativity.

This presence did not guarantee harmony. It guaranteed honesty.

Honesty deepened relationships that could hold it. It clarified relationships that could not. In both cases, acceptance provided clarity rather than confusion.

In both cases, the acceptance brought clarity and not confusion.

I also observed that acceptance made a difference in the way that I responded to my own changes in emotional states. Earlier, I had tried to correct them. Now, I allowed them to pass. This allowance made them less intense.

When I stopped asking emotional consistency out of myself, I stopped asking it out of others.

This symmetry mattered.

I began seeing relationships not as static bonds but as evolving interactions. Some grew closer. Some drifted. Some transformed into something else entirely. Acceptance allowed these movements without resistance.

Resistance freezes relationships. Acceptance lets them breathe.

This breathing space reduced drama. It reduced unnecessary attachment. It allowed appreciation without possession.

As this understanding settled, the mirror reflected something new. It reflected a self less invested in control and more invested in clarity. Less results-oriented and more process-oriented.

This reflection was not self-congratulatory. It was steady.

Steadiness replaced intensity.

And in that steadiness, judgment matured naturally.

As acceptance came more naturally, I started seeing how expectations fell away without exerting any effort. Earlier, I tried to consciously control expectations. I told myself not to expect too much. I tried to be reasonable. But expectation does not disappear through intention. It dissolves when perception matures.

Expectation survives on resistance.

When I resisted reality, expectation stayed alive. When I accepted reality, expectation lost its footing. I no longer needed people to behave a certain way for me to feel balanced. This was not to say that

I had no preferences. It meant preferences no longer ruled perception.

This changed how I related to first impressions.

Earlier, first impressions felt important because expectations were active. I wanted clarity quickly. I wanted to know where I stood. I wanted to decide how much to invest. First impressions offered temporary certainty.

Now, certainty felt less urgent.

First impressions still arose, but they felt lighter. I noticed them without believing them completely. They became impressions, not conclusions. Signals, not statements.

This difference mattered.

When I stopped clinging to first impressions, people didn't feel so trapped. I did not downgrade them to what I saw at first. I allowed them to contradict me without feeling threatened. I allowed myself to revise my understanding without shame.

Revision became natural.

Truth, I realised, is not something we possess. It is something we approach. When we cling to truth too tightly, it becomes hard as belief. When we go near it gently, it is still alive.

Acceptance keeps truth fluid.

This fluidity did not make me indecisive. It made me accurate. I was no longer defending old perceptions. I was responding to what was there in the present moment. When new information arrived, perception updated quietly.

This quiet update changed how I experienced trust.

Earlier, trust felt risky. It required certainty. I trusted people when my impressions felt strong. When impressions wavered, trust collapsed. Acceptance reshaped this dynamic.

Trust no longer depended on impressions. It depended on patterns over time. Consistency. Behavior across contexts. Reactions under pressure and ease.

Trust slowed down.

Slowness protected clarity.

I also noticed how acceptance reshaped disappointment. Earlier, disappointment felt personal. Someone had failed me. Something had gone wrong. Now, disappointment felt informational. An expectation had revealed itself.

Disappointment stopped accusing others. It pointed inward.

This inward turn was not self-blame. It was self-awareness. I could see where imagination had overreached. Where hope had filled gaps prematurely. Where expectation had replaced observation.

This awareness softened disappointment quickly.

Without expectation, disappointment loses intensity.

I also noticed how acceptance changed my relationship with hope. Hope no longer clung to outcomes. It became openness. Openness to what unfolds rather than insistence on what should.

This openness felt calm.

Earlier, calm felt boring. Now, it felt stable. Calm did not dull the experience. It refined it. I could enjoy connection without clinging. I could appreciate moments without demanding permanence.

This impermanence no longer felt threatening.

Acceptance had changed how I understood impermanence. Earlier, impermanence felt like loss. Now, it felt like movement. Movement allowed growth. Growth allowed understanding.

Understanding replaced attachment.

I also noticed how acceptance changed the way I held my own beliefs. Earlier, beliefs felt like anchors. Now, they felt like reference points. Useful but adjustable. Helpful but not absolute.

This flexibility did not weaken integrity. It strengthened it. Integrity built on acceptance does not fear revision. It welcomes correction.

Correction refined perception.

As beliefs loosened, ego softened further. The ego had earlier protected certainty. Now, it had less to protect. Identity no longer depended on being right. It rested in being aware.

This resting felt expansive.

With ego softened, interactions felt less charged. I no longer felt the need to win conversations. I did not need to impress. I did not need to dominate. Presence was enough.

Presence invited presence.

People often mirrored this unconsciously. Conversations became slower. More thoughtful. Less performative. Even silence felt comfortable.

This comfort allowed deeper seeing.

I also noticed how acceptance changed the way I processed feedback. Earlier, feedback felt evaluative. Now, it felt descriptive. I could hear criticism without collapsing. I could receive praise without being inflated.

Balance emerged.

Balance did not flatten emotion. It stabilized it. I could feel fully without being carried away.

As this balance settled, perception reached a quiet maturity. Not dramatic insight. Not heightened intuition. But a steady clarity that did not rush to conclude.

I realised that accuracy in judgment does not come from seeing more. It comes from interfering less.

Acceptance reduces interference.

When interference reduces, reality reveals itself naturally. People show their patterns. Situations clarify. Truth does not need force.

This was perhaps the deepest shift. I stopped trying to understand life. I allowed life to show itself.

This allowance did not make me passive. It made me attentive.

Attentiveness replaced vigilance.

Vigilance looks for threats. Attentiveness looks for truth.

Acceptance transformed one into the other.

As everything settled, I began noticing something that felt almost anticlimactic. There was no final insight. No dramatic conclusion. No moment where life suddenly announced that clarity had arrived.

Instead, clarity felt ordinary.

It appeared in how little effort it now took to understand situations that once felt complex. It showed up in how rarely I felt the urge to defend myself. It lived in the way first impressions passed through me without asking for belief.

The mirror no longer reflected ambition or insecurity. It reflected alignment.

Looking into the mirror with acceptance did not mean liking everything I saw. It meant not quarrelling with what was there. It meant recognising patterns without turning them into problems. It meant seeing limitation without turning it into identity.

In that honesty, compassion stabilised.

Compassion no longer felt selective. I did not need to decide who deserved it. When resistance ended, compassion became the natural response to seeing clearly. Not pity. Not softness. Just understanding without distortion.

This understanding reshaped conviction.

Conviction no longer came from certainty. It came from steadiness. I could have a perspective and not be attached to it. I was able to voice an opinion without having to have it accepted. I could walk away with no feeling of being diminished.

This forbearance didn't keep me from fellowships. It helped me relate better to people.

When I stopped trying to correct people, I heard them better. When I stopped taking things personally, conversations were light. When I stopped rushing to get things over with, relationships were revealed more fully.

First impressions lost their urgency.

They still arrived. They always will. But they arrived as whispers rather than commands. They introduced, not defined. They suggested, not decided.

This was the quiet collapse of the myth.

First impressions were never wrong. They were never right either. They were simply early.

And early does not mean accurate.

Accuracy arrives with patience, awareness, and acceptance working together. Not as techniques, but as a way of being. When the inner resistance dissolves, perception aligns naturally.

Life stops needing interpretation. It begins to feel legible.

I also noticed that acceptance softened how I experienced others' flaws. Earlier, flaws stood out sharply. Now, they blended into context. I could see where someone struggled without reducing them to that struggle. I could recognise strength without exaggeration.

This balance felt humane.

Humane perception does not idolise or demonise. It sees proportion. It recognises that everyone is negotiating something invisible. That behavior is often a surface expression of deeper movement.

When this recognition stabilised, judgment matured fully. It no longer arrived as a reaction. It arrived as discernment. Calm, delayed, informed.

Discernment guided by acceptance does not rush. It waits until understanding feels complete enough to act. And even then, it remains open to revision.

Revision stopped feeling like failure. It felt like intelligence adapting.

I realised then that the most accurate judgments are rarely loud. They do not announce themselves with certainty. They feel quiet, settled, almost unremarkable.

That quietness is their strength.

As I look back now, it becomes clear that this entire journey was never about learning how to judge others better. It was about learning how to see myself clearly enough that others no longer needed to be filtered through distortion.

When I stopped fighting my own inner movements, the world stopped feeling combative. When I stopped demanding coherence from myself, I stopped demanding it from others.

Acceptance did not blur perception.

It sharpened it.

Not by adding information, but by removing noise.

And once the noise reduced, something simple became obvious.

First impressions were never the problem. Resistance was.

When resistance dissolved, perception matured naturally. The mirror reflected what was always there. A self-capable of awareness. A self-capable of acceptance. A self-capable of seeing without rushing to define.

That is when empathy stops being an effort. That is when compassion stops being chosen. That is when clarity stops being chased.

It simply remains.

And in that remaining, the world feels quieter, wider, and more complete than it ever did before.

Chapter 9: Beyond First Impressions – Living with Clarity

When you started this book, I asked you to stop and answer a few questions.

Simple questions. Direct ones. Questions about how you see people. How quickly you judge. What you believe about first impressions.

At that time, you were answering from wherever you were standing.

Today, before you read another word, I want you to jump back to those answers. Not to criticize them. Not to correct them. Just to look at them again.

Read them slowly.

Notice the tone.

Notice the certainty.

Notice the assumptions hidden inside what felt obvious.

The surprise was never dramatic. It was never meant to shock you. It was meant to reveal something quieter.

You have changed.

Or at the very least, your way of looking has.

First impressions feel powerful because they arrive before understanding. They are fast, emotional, and convincing. They do not wait for evidence. They do not ask for context. They simply appear and demand belief.

Over time, those impressions do something subtle. They transform into expectations.

An early assumption becomes a silent rule.

"This is how this person is."

"This is how this situation will unfold."

"This is what I can expect from them."

The moment expectation is formed, suffering begins to take root. Not because reality is cruel, but because reality rarely aligns perfectly with imagination.

We do not suffer because people are wrong. We suffer because our expectations feel right.

And when expectation collides with truth, we defend expectation.

This has been the uncomfortable thread running quietly through every chapter of this book. First impressions are not lasting. They are temporary conclusions drawn from limited information. But when we fail to revisit them, they harden. They settle into belief. And belief begins to dictate how we see.

Relationships suffer not because people are inherently flawed, but because expectations spawned by initial impressions are accepted as permanent truths.

We expect partners to be consistent with the version that we first admired. We expect friends to behave according to the role we gave them. We expect parents to stand still in the images that we created years ago. We expect children to grow along the path we imagined.

When they evolve, we resist.

When they reveal complexity, we feel betrayed.

When they disappoint the version we constructed, we blame them for changing.

But it is not change that hurts.

It is an attachment to the earlier impression.

Our expectations are not universal guidelines. They are individual interpretations formed by memory, bias, conditioning, and emotion. Yet we act as if our expectations are the laws of morality. When others don't do what we want, we feel wronged.

Disappointment turns into frustration. Frustration turns into conflict. Conflict becomes distance.

And all of it started with a first impression that we never changed.

First impressions are powerful, but they are only thoughts formed in a moment. They feel permanent because we mistake speed for truth. A glance becomes a judgment. A moment becomes a label. A single experience becomes a definition. But thoughts are not foundations. They are interpretations.

"I think, therefore I am" suggests that thinking defines existence. If this is true, then every impression, ours or someone else's, gains dangerous authority. We begin to live inside conclusions formed too quickly. We allow momentary thoughts to decide lasting identities.

I see it differently.

I exist; therefore, I think.

Existence comes first. Before opinions. Before assumptions. Before praise or criticism. There is simply being. Thoughts arise from that being, and thoughts can change. When thinking changes, impressions must change too. What is formed in seconds cannot imprison what was formed by existence itself.

A first impression is not destiny. It is not a character. It is not the truth carved in stone. It is a temporary mental event.

If I exist before I think, then no single thought can define me forever.

And if that is true for me, it is true for everyone.

First impressions are not lasting, because existence always outlives perception.

If we could bring expectation to reality and not force reality to change to be what we expect it to be, then a lot of our suffering would melt away. But this is hard to do because we are so invested in our way of seeing.

The life that we live is the life that we live right now because it's what we're used to. Familiarity is a source of comfort, even when it limits growth.

Indian philosophy addresses this inner conflict in ways that are timeless.

In a scene in the Bhagavad Gita, Arjuna is standing on the battlefield, overwhelmed. His crisis is not about skill. It is not about courage. It is about perception. His first impression of the situation turns out to be his permanent belief. He sees only loss. Only attachment. Only emotional devastation.

He expects life to conform to his comfort and confusion.

When it does not, he collapses inwards.

Krishna does not alter the location of the battle. He does not take responsibility away. He changes perception. He shifts Arjuna's perspective from being attached to being dutiful, from being fearful to clear. Once perception changes, action is possible.

The war remained the same.

Arjuna did not.

In the Ramayana, a powerful moment unfolds when Jamwant reminds Hanuman of the extraordinary strength he has long forgotten. Until that pivotal encounter, Hanuman sees himself merely as one of the vanaras, capable yet far from exceptional. However, Jamwant's words act like a mirror, reflecting Hanuman's true potential back to him. In that instant, the shadows of self-doubt lift, and Hanuman's self-perception transforms dramatically; he shifts from viewing himself as an ordinary being to recognizing the mighty force he is destined to be.

Nothing in his surroundings changes, but his awareness does, and that inner awakening alters the trajectory of history itself. The leap to Lanka transcends mere physical action; it symbolizes a profound journey from uncertainty to unwavering belief, from hesitation to purposeful resolve. Today, we honor Hanuman not just for his remarkable strength, but for that transformative moment of self-realization. Sometimes, true greatness isn't something we acquire; it's something we awaken from within.

These stories are not distant mythology. They are psychological mirrors. They reveal a simple truth. What binds us is not inability. It is an attachment to outdated impressions.

In real life, no Krishna walks beside us daily. No Jamwant appears to remind us of hidden strength. The responsibility to outgrow first impressions lies with us.

And that responsibility is not dramatic.

It is disciplined.

Change rarely begins with revelation. It begins with observation. Honest, discomforting observation. Where are my expectations coming from? What beliefs have I been making long ago but never re-examined? Where am I justifying something because it has always been there?

Finding oneself is not an instant. It is practice.

As we practice, resistance appears. The version of ourselves that we are adopted, the version of ourselves that is shaped by habit and conditioning, doesn't step aside easily. It drags us back towards the known.

This is why so many resolutions fade. Every year, people begin with clarity and intention. By February, enthusiasm weakens. We admire those who sustain change and call them disciplined. But discipline is not extraordinary. It is structure.

Discipline is loyalty to growth when excitement is over.

When desire to change comes from within, discipline is natural and easy. One of the easiest ways to develop this desire is journaling. Writing exposes patterns. It prevents impressions of ourselves from hardening into identity.

When I write consistently, I catch myself in repetition. I notice where I am clinging. I see where expectation is shaping perception.

Journaling does not change me instantly. It keeps awareness alive.

And awareness keeps perception fluid.

At the deepest level, self-improvement is compassion. Not self-criticism. Not self-reinvention. Compassion.

When I soften myself towards my own blind spots, I soften myself towards yours. When I let my perception change, I let yours change.

Money, relationships, harmony, friendship. These are not trophies. They are byproducts. Byproducts of clarity. Byproducts of compassion.

When first impressions lose authority, understanding begins. When expectations loosen, relationships breathe. When perception shifts, life opens.

There is an image that has stayed with me.

Two people stand in front of a mirror. The mirror reflects exactly what is there. No preference. No judgment. Just truth.

One person lifts a pillow and holds it in front of his own face. From his position, the mirror appears empty. He cannot see himself. He assumes nothing is being reflected.

The other person steps slightly to the side. From a different angle, he sees the reflection clearly. He sees the man behind the pillow. He sees the expression. The confusion.

To the man holding the pillow, this feels impossible. He wonders how the mirror knows something he cannot see.

But there is no magic in the mirror.

Reality does not hide.

We block our own view.

Life works in the same way. What we see depends on our position within it.

If we refuse to shift position, we call the truth a distortion. If we step aside, clarity appears.

You can know 90 percent about a person or a situation. Patterns. History. Words. Even intention. But the remaining 10 percent is not just missing data. It is uncertainty. Timing. Emotion. Evolution.

That 10 percent can change everything.

"I may understand most of a person, yet the part I don't know is what changes everything."

Knowing is never complete. Awareness includes knowing the limits of your knowing. Certainty reduces perception. Humility expands it.

I have learned that I can be 90 percent right and absolutely wrong.

This humility is not weakness. It is clarity.

When you look back at your answers to the Reflection Test, I do not want you to judge yourself. I want you to notice the shift. Perhaps earlier, you believed first impressions were reliable. Perhaps you defended intuition strongly. Perhaps you were confident in your reading of people.

Now, read those answers again.

Has anything softened?

Has certainty loosened?

Has curiosity replaced conclusion?

If yes, then perception has matured.

The surprise was never external.

It was you.

Beyond first impressions lies something quieter. A way of living where clarity replaces urgency. Where reflection replaces reaction. Where understanding grows because expectation no longer demands compliance.

Living with clarity does not imply abandoning discernment. It means refining it. It means letting the perception evolve, rather than defending it. It means accepting that people are processes and not static definitions.

First impressions are not permanent, but only if we decide not to live off of them.

The moment we let perception change; we enter the realm of freedom.

Freedom from defending outdated beliefs. Freedom from punishing others for not matching one's imagination. Freedom from freezing ourselves in earlier versions.

Living with clarity is not about seeing perfectly. It is about seeing honestly. It is about knowing that what you see today may not be complete. It is about remaining open to revision.

And perhaps that is the quiet ending of this journey.

Not a conclusion.

An invitation.

To keep observing. To keep updating. To keep softening certainty into awareness.

The mirror, normally, has always been clear.

The only question is, will we be willing to change our position long enough to, see?

Verses Kindler Publication

Verses Kindler Publication

Reach us through our website -

https://www.verseskindlerpublication.com/

For more information visit our

Instagram or Facebook page.